CONTEMPORARY'S

Make Your Mark
in Retail Jobs

ROSEMARY GREBEL

PHYLLIS POGRUND

CONTEMPORARY
BOOKS

A DIVISION OF NTC/CONTEMPORARY
PUBLISHING COMPANY

Manufactured in the United States of America
International Standard Book Number: 0-8092-0910-1
7 8 9 B A 0 9 8 7 6 5 4 3 2 1

Market Development Manager
Noreen Lopez

Editorial Development Director
Cynthia Krejcsi

Project Manager
Laurie Duncan

Editorial
Carlos Byfield

Production
Thomas D. Scharf

Cover Design
Michael Kelly

Production Artist
Kristy Sheldon

Line Art Illustrations
David Will

Contents

Dear Student,

Welcome to *Make Your Mark in Retail Jobs.* This book can help you learn on-the-job English, as well as strategies for advancement, in many retail settings.

The retail industry always needs workers with the right skills. *Make Your Mark in Retail Jobs* teaches the vocabulary and information needed to perform various retail jobs, from stock clerk to catalog sales associate. With this book, you can practice actual conversations to use on the job. Learn how to talk to customers, co-workers, and managers. Discover how to work cooperatively for success as a team member. Find out what it takes to become a manager.

The skills in this book provide helpful information that apply to many areas of the retail industry and to stores both large and small. Much of the book is set at Davis and Landau, an imaginary department store. At Davis and Landau, you can see how a large retail business operates and promotes good workers.

If you are interested in a retail career, this book will help you get started. We hope you enjoy the lessons, and we wish you much success.

Rosemary Grebel
Phyllis Pogrund

Unit 1
NO WAITING ON REGISTER THREE!

Who are the people in the picture above? What are the two workers doing? What words below might describe what they are doing?

Words to Know

aisle	miss	total	low
bar code	nail polish	voice	next
candy	price		rainy
cash register	product	(to) buy	though
change	purchase	(to) charge	unadvertised
cosmetic	scanner	(to) check	
counter	second	(to) clean	quickly
customer	shopper	(to) include	
glass	sir	(to) input	
go-back	special	(to) keep (someone)	excuse me
go-back	special	waiting	great!
item	store	(to) put	in a hurry
line	tax	(something) back	kind of
ma'am	toothbrush	(to) sign	no problem

Listen and Speak

Step 1: Listen as your teacher reads the conversations between Laura and her customers.

Laura:	There's no waiting on register three.
Customer 1:	OK, great. Here are my items.
Laura:	How are you on this rainy night, ma'am?
Customer 1:	Just fine, thanks, but I'm kind of in a hurry.
Laura:	OK. I'll check you through quickly. Uh-oh, my scanner isn't reading the bar code. I have to input the numbers on the cash register. I'll try to be fast.
Customer 2:	[*in line*] No, Kevin, no candy today. Put it back.
Kevin:	Aw, Mom, please!
Laura:	[*to Customer 1*] I'm sorry to keep you waiting. That's $6.47 including tax. [*takes ten dollars from customer*] Out of ten. [*counts change and gives it to customer*] That's $6.47, 48, 49, 50, 7, 8, 9, and 10 dollars. Thank you for shopping at SavMorCo. Have a nice evening.
Customer 3:	Excuse me. Where are the toothbrushes?
Laura:	They're in aisle 16B, sir, in the back of the store. [*to customer in line*] Next?
Customer 2:	We're next, Kevin. Put your candy on the counter, so I can pay for it.
Laura:	Just one second, please. I have to clean the glass on the scanner.
Voice:	Attention, shoppers. There's an unadvertised special on all our cosmetic products in aisles 6 and 7. Always low, low prices at SavMorCo!
Customer 2:	I'm going to check the cosmetics. Let's go, Kevin.
Laura:	OK. I'll see you later. May I help the next person in line, please?
Customer 4:	Here are my purchases. I don't want to buy this nail polish, though.
Laura:	OK, that's no problem. I'll put it with the go-backs. [*rings up purchases*] Your total is $18.92.
Customer 4:	I want to charge it. Do you take the Topcard?
Laura:	Yes, we do. [*takes customer's card*] Thank you. [*hands credit slip to customer*] OK, please sign on this line.
Customer 4:	OK. Thanks.
Laura:	Thank you for shopping at SavMorCo. Please come again. Good night.

Step 2: Read the conversations with a partner.

Step 3: Discuss these questions with your partner.

- What did Laura do when the scanner did not read the bar code? Why?
- Do you think Laura is a good worker? Why?

Step 1: Read the sentences. Match each sentence on the left with the correct sentence that follows it on the right. The first one is done for you.

1. My scanner isn't reading the bar code.
2. I don't want this nail polish.
3. No candy today.
4. Where are the toothbrushes?

a. Put it back.
b. I'll input the numbers.
c. In aisle 16B.
d. I'll put it with the go-backs.

Step 2: Place the correct word from the box under each picture below.

bar code	scanner
cash register	shoppers
counter	store

1.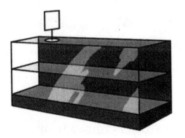

4.

2.

5.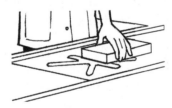

3.

6.

0 123456 789128

Unit 1: No Waiting on Register Three!   3

Build Your Vocabulary

SavMorCo! The Place You Love To Shop!

Words to Know

activity	(to) appeal	nonselling
ad	(to) belong	seasonal
appeal	(to) handle	terrific
cart	(to) hurry	give a hand
chain	(to) pick up	good for you!
coupon	(to) remember	in other words
display	(to) run	out of place
manager	(in an ad)	thanks to you
meeting	(to) set up	to-do list
news	(to) shop	
number one		
ourselves		
service	attractive	
team	neat	

Step 1: Read what the manager says at the meeting.

"Good morning. First, I've got great news! Thanks to you, our store is number one in the chain! Let's give ourselves a hand. We have got a terrific team here! Good for all of you! You're doing great.

Here on the wall is our new ad with specials for the week. Please notice the coupons we're running. New seasonal products are coming in, too. Here are some of them on this cart. You'll have time to look at all of these products, so you can answer customer questions.

Check your to-do lists. Some of you will help me set up the seasonal display for the front of the store. We want it to look great. As we always say here, 'Eye appeal is buy appeal.' In other words, if it appeals to the eye, the customer will buy it. Some of you will handle go-backs. Pick them up at the registers often and put them back where they belong. Everyone, please pick up products that are out of place and put them back. We want our store to look neat and attractive! But if you're doing nonselling activities and hear your name, hurry to open your register. We have to help customers as much as we can.

Remember, this is the place customers love to shop. Our good service is why they come here! Do you have any questions? No? Well, have a great day!"

Step 2: Work with a partner. Discuss these questions.

- The manager says, "Eye appeal is buy appeal." What do you think this means?

- Why do you think SavMorCo workers work together as a team?

Step 1: Place a check mark next to the statements that are true.

_____ 1. The manager is happy with the workers at the store.

_____ 2. This SavMorCo store is the only one there is.

_____ 3. It is important to work together as a team at the store.

_____ 4. There is a new ad with new specials every day.

_____ 5. Workers must learn what the seasonal products are.

_____ 6. A to-do list is a list of jobs the manager must do.

_____ 7. Customers set up displays in the front of the store.

_____ 8. Go-backs are products that customers do not want to buy.

_____ 9. Customers go to the store because it has good customer service.

Step 2: Fill in the blanks with words from the story.

Here on the wall is our new _____ with specials for the week. Please notice

the _____ we're running. New _____ products are coming

in, too. Here are some of them on this cart. You'll have time to look at all of these products,

so you can answer customer _____.

Check your _____ lists. Some of you will help me set up the seasonal

_____ for the front of the store. We want it to look _____.

As we always say here, "_____ appeal is _____ appeal."

In other words, if it _____ to the eye, the customer will buy it.

Some of you will handle _____. Pick them up at the _____

often and put them back where they _____. Everyone, please

_____ products that are out of place and _____ them back.

We want our _____ to look neat and attractive! But if you're doing

nonselling activities and hear your _____, hurry to _____

your register. We have to _____ customers as much as we can.

Listen and Speak

Words to Know

button	roll of film	(to) sound	between
buy	warranty	(to) shoot	
camera	zoom lens	(to) take (pictures)	Do you see what I mean?
case			
difference	(to) advertise	automatic	for the money
feature	(to) carry	both	How about . . . ?
flash	(to) come with	built-in	How much . . . ?
focus	(to) finish	excellent	I'll take it.
photograph (photo)	(to) cost	lightweight	point and shoot
pocket	(to) get		You sold me on it.
promotion (promo)	(to) hold		
rewind	(to) push		

Step 1:   Listen as your teacher reads the conversation.

Greg: Hello. How are you today?

Customer: Fine, thanks. I'd like to see the camera you advertised.

Greg: Was that the Techi or the Nice Shot camera? They're both in our ad.

Customer: Could I see them both? What are the differences between them?

Greg: This is the Techi. It is an automatic focus model with built-in flash. It's very lightweight. Here, hold it. Do you see?

Customer: Yes. I can carry this one in my pocket. Now, how about the Nice Shot?

Greg: This one also is a lightweight "point and shoot" camera, but it has more features. It has automatic rewind and a zoom lens. Do you see what I mean?

Customer: Yes. Do I just push this button for the zoom lens and this one to shoot?

Greg: Yes. And the Nice Shot comes with a camera case and two rolls of film.

Customer: The Techi doesn't come with those things? And how much does it cost?

Greg: No, only the Nice Shot is a promo this week. It costs $84.99 for everything. That's a great buy for the money. It also has a two-year warranty.

Customer: Well, it sounds excellent. You sold me on it. I'll take it.

Greg: Great! I'll get you one in a box.

Step 2:   Read the dialogue with another student.

Step 3:   Why do you think Greg gave the cameras to the customer to hold? Discuss your answer with your partner.

Practice

Step 1: Circle the letter of the answer that best completes each sentence.

1. Greg begins his sales by saying,
   a. "May I help you?"
   b. "How are you today?"
   c. "How may I help you?"

2. Greg shows the customer
   a. one camera.
   b. two cameras.
   c. three cameras.

3. The two cameras are almost the same, but one of them
   a. has more features.
   b. costs more money.
   c. is lightweight.

4. When Greg talks about the features, he
   a. takes some pictures.
   b. gives the camera to the customer to hold.
   c. says, "Great! I'll get you one in a box."

Step 2: Pretend that you are a camera salesclerk. Fill in what you would say in the conversation below.

You: _____

Customer: Fine, thanks. I'd like to see the camera in your ad.

You: _____

Customer: Could I see them both? What are the differences between them?

You: _____

Customer: Yes, I see. Now, how about the other one?

You: _____

Customer: Do I just push this button?

You: _____

Customer: And it has more features than the Techi? How much does it cost?

You: _____

Customer: Well, it sounds excellent. You sold me on it. I'll take it.

You: _____

Step 3: Practice the conversation you just wrote with a partner.

Be a Good Worker

Step 1: Listen as your teacher reads the information on the TV screen. It is from a videotape for new workers.

- Always be early or on time for work.
- Take your breaks when your manager tells you to take them.
- Look your best. Follow our dress code.
- Keep your hair clean and your fingernails short.
- Never eat, chew gum, drink, or smoke while working.
- Smile at customers, make good eye contact, and always be polite.
- Keep busy. Work on your to-do list when you are not helping customers.
- Remember that giving good customer service is your number-one job!

Step 2: Circle the pictures below that show good workers.

1.

3.

Clock in ten minutes before the hour.

2.

4.

Have Some Fun!

Step 1: The scrambled words below also appear in the word box on this page. Unscramble the words and write them on the lines below.

1. yee _____

2. aappel _____

3. yub _____

4. sidylap _____

5. mate _____

6. grestier _____

7. sutcerom _____

8. perpsho _____

9. og-skacb _____

10. furteae _____

attractive	customer	handle	register
automatic	display	input	scanner
buy appeal	eye appeal	manager	shopper
clean up	feature	meeting	special
counter	glass	products	team
credit card	go-backs	purchase	unadvertised

Step 2: Find the words from the box in the puzzle below. The words may be horizontal, vertical, or diagonal. They may even be backward. Circle the words you find.

E	S	A	H	C	R	U	P	U	N	A	E	L	C	A	J	D
F	M	O	G	V	L	N	F	I	Q	G	N	I	T	E	E	M
B	E	V	I	T	C	A	R	T	T	A	K	H	A	L	R	Z
G	R	I	A	J	U	D	I	R	E	G	A	N	A	M	G	P
O	C	P	N	X	T	V	S	C	A	N	N	E	R	L	R	R
B	U	Y	A	P	P	E	A	L	E	C	P	Y	S	O	E	E
A	T	L	I	Q	U	R	Y	N	D	P	A	C	D	M	T	G
C	I	T	A	M	O	T	U	A	A	L	S	U	O	E	N	I
K	U	E	V	K	N	I	M	E	P	D	C	T	X	L	U	S
S	S	A	L	G	Y	S	Y	S	B	T	S	E	K	D	O	T
F	E	A	T	U	R	E	I	W	S	U	O	Z	A	N	C	E
B	W	P	C	R	E	D	I	T	C	A	R	D	S	A	H	R
T	E	A	M	H	I	E	S	G	R	E	P	P	O	H	S	F

Think It Over

Step 1: Sometimes workers open a sales conversation with a greeting. On page 6, Greg started his camera sale by saying, "Hello. How are you today?" This is an example of a greeting. On each line below, write *Yes* if the words greet a customer and *No* if they do not.

1. _____ Hello. How are you today?

2. _____ Hi. Nice day, isn't it?

3. _____ Those socks are good for cold weather.

4. _____ Good morning.

5. _____ I can help the next person in line, please.

6. _____ That button is for the flash.

7. _____ There's no waiting on register three.

8. _____ Good evening. How are you doing tonight?

Step 2: Read the information below in a group of three or four students.

Workers often tell customers about the features of a product. Some features are easy to see. If a camera is small, that is an easy-to-see feature. Other features, such as a built-in flash, are not easy to see.

The benefits, or helpful features, of a product are also important things for workers to tell customers. "It can fit into your pocket," is a benefit of a small camera.

Step 3: Pretend that your group is going to sell the products below. Think of some features and benefits that will help you sell each product. On another piece of paper, make a list of features and benefits for each product.

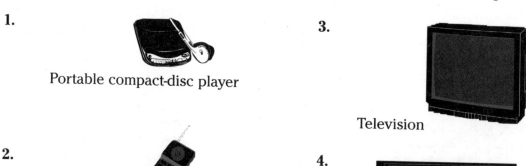

1.

Portable compact-disc player

2.

Cellular phone

3.

Television

4.

Video cassette recorder

Check Your Understanding

Step 1: **Draw lines to connect the sentences that go together.**

1. The scanner is not reading the bar code.

2. This is the place customers love to shop.

3. We've got a terrific team.

4. Eye appeal is buy appeal.

5. You will handle go-backs.

6. This one has more features for the money.

7. Work on your to-do list.

8. How are you doing?

a. We work well together and help each other.

b. If it appeals to the eye, the customer will buy it.

c. I have to input the numbers on the register.

d. It is a great buy. I'll take it.

e. Do this when you are not helping customers.

f. Pick items up often at the registers and put them back on the shelf.

g. Fine, thanks.

h. Our good service is why customers come here.

Step 2: **Read what the customer says. Circle the best response for the worker to give.**

1. I'm kind of in a hurry.
   a. May I help the next person in line, please?
   b. OK. I'll check you through quickly.
   c. Thank you very much. Have a good evening.

2. I don't want to buy the toothbrush.
   a. Can I give you a hand?
   b. Put it back.
   c. That's no problem. I'll put it with the go-backs.

3. I want to charge it. Here's my Topcard.
   a. Thank you. Please sign on this line.
   b. OK. Put it back.
   c. No problem.

4. I'd like to see the camera you advertised.
   a. Do you see what I mean?
   b. It has automatic rewind and a zoom lens.
   c. This is the Big Shot in our ad. Here, hold it.

5. How much does it cost?
   a. It's 5:45 P.M.
   b. It's $24.99.
   c. That's 50 cents, 7, 8, 9, and 10 dollars.

6. Well, I'll take it.
   a. OK. I'll get you one in a box.
   b. Do you see what I mean?
   c. You sold me on it!

Try It!

Complete the first activity in class. Then do activity 2 on your own.

1. Work with a small group of students. Discuss these questions:
   - Do you ever shop in a store like SavMorCo? Compare the workers at SavMorCo with the workers at the store where you shop.
   - Would you like to work in a store like SavMorCo? Why?
   - Do you think coupons are a good idea for saving money? Do you use coupons? Why? Why not?
   - Do you ever notice or buy products that are in store displays? Do you believe "Eye appeal is buy appeal"? Explain.
   - The products such as candy that stores place near the registers are called "impulse items." Why do you think they are called impulse items?

2. Go to a SavMorCo type of store near your home and then answer these questions. Share your answers with the class.
   - In what ways is the store like SavMorCo? In what ways is it different?
   - Were the workers at the store like the workers in this unit? How were they the same or different?
   - Did the workers at the store work as a team?
   - Did you see any displays of seasonal products? Did you see displays of other products?
   - Were the workers friendly to customers?
   - Did the workers smile when they made a sales approach?
   - Do you think service to the customer is important in that store?

Notes

_____

_____

_____

_____

_____

_____

_____

_____

_____

Unit 2
LOOKING FOR ANYTHING SPECIAL?

Look at the picture. Where are the people? What do you think they are talking about? What words are pictured that also appear in the word box?

Words to Know

back	salesperson	(to) decide	large
cash	shelf	(to) look for	medium
clothes	size	(to) meet	striped
fitting room	style	(to) show	
food court	men's department	(to) split up	especially
juniors' department		(to) try on	
rack	(to) come in (a style		just looking
receipt	or color)		right back

Listen and Speak

Step 1:   Listen as your teacher reads the conversation. Cherice and Tom are customers at a store. Rajid is a salesperson.

Tom: Cherice, you want to go to the juniors' department, and I need to go to men's. Let's split up and meet in the food court in two hours. Then we can show each other what we've bought.

Cherice: OK. That's a good idea. See you in two hours in the food court.

LATER, IN THE STORE

Rajid: Good morning. May I help you?

Tom: No, thanks. I'm just looking.

Rajid: Oh. Are you looking for anything special?

Tom: Yeah. I'm looking for school clothes, especially shirts.

Rajid: Our new line is on these racks. What size shirt do you wear?

Tom: Usually medium. Do you have this blue striped one in medium?

Rajid: We may. There are more in the back. I'll check on it for you. Is there anything else you want me to look for in back?

Tom: Yes, please. I like this style, but I don't like green. Will you see if you have any other colors in my size? And where's the fitting room to try these on?

Rajid: I think they only come in those colors on the shelf, but I'll check. You can try them on over here. Also, these pants look especially good with that style of shirt. [*hands Tom some pants*] I'll be right back.

LATER

Rajid: Have you decided?

Tom: Yes. I'll take these three shirts, this underwear, and this pair of pants.

Rajid: Good. Will that be cash or charge?

Tom: Cash.

Rajid: OK. That will be $62.58, including tax. [*takes $65.00 from Tom*] Out of $65.00. Your change is $2.42. Your receipt is in the bag. Thank you for shopping at Davis and Landau. Good-bye.

Step 2:   Read the conversation with a partner.

Step 3:   With your partner, discuss the following questions:
   • Why does Rajid want to know if Tom is looking for anything special?
   • Do you think Rajid is a good salesperson? Why?

Practice

Step 1: Read the questions below and write your answers on the lines. If you need help, read the conversation on page 14 again.

1. What is the first question that Rajid asks Tom?

_____

_____

2. To help Tom find the clothes he wants, what does Rajid offer to do?

_____

_____

3. What does Rajid ask to find out how Tom will pay for his purchases?

_____

_____

4. To get Tom to buy more items, what does Rajid say?

_____

_____

Step 2: Write *True* if the sentence is true and *False* if it is false.

_____ 1. Rajid is a helpful salesperson.

_____ 2. Rajid asks no questions if the customers are "just looking."

_____ 3. Rajid shows Tom more kinds of clothes than he is looking for.

_____ 4. Tom wants to buy shoes and shirts.

_____ 5. Tom is shopping in the boy's department.

Step 3: Pretend that you are a salesperson like Rajid. Fill in what you would say in the conversation below. Then practice the conversation with a partner.

You: _____

Customer: No, thanks. I'm just looking.

You: _____

Customer: [*pointing to a sweater*] I'm looking for this style of sweater.

You: _____

Customer: Size large, if you have it.

You: _____

Customer: Yes. Please check on it. Thanks.

Build Your Vocabulary

Words to Know

accessory	handbag	salesclerk	floating
appliance	lingerie	sales technique	interested
break	lunch	staff	ready
costume jewelry	merchandise		smart
curling iron	object	(to) cover	
directory	patron	(to) explain	for example
electric knife	selection	(to) touch	
electronics	sales associate		

Step 1: Read about Elise's job.

Elise works at Davis and Landau as a floating sales associate. She covers breaks and lunches for the other salesclerks. That means she works in many departments. She often works in electronics, toys, lingerie, costume jewelry, housewares, handbags and accessories, and juniors. Elise likes her job. She is interested in the different products in each department. She knows something about the products in each department.

Elise uses many sales techniques to sell different merchandise. For example, if she is selling a small appliance like an electric knife, she lets the customer hold the object as she explains its features. When she is selling clothes, Elise offers to keep a patron's selections until he or she is ready to try them on.

Elise knows that if a customer touches an item or picks it up, he or she is interested in it. So, she offers to help when a patron is interested in an item. She's a smart salesclerk.

Step 2: Work with a partner. Answer the following questions about Elise:
- Why do you think Elise wants the customer to handle the product?
- Why is Elise a smart salesclerk?

Practice

Step 1: Look at the pictures and the departments listed in the box. Under each picture, write the name of the department where you can find that item.

toys	lingerie
small appliances	electronics
handbags and accessories	men's

1. _____

2. _____

3. _____

4. _____

5. _____

6. _____

Step 2: Read each item below. Place a check mark next to the items that show good sales techniques.

_____ 1. A customer in the lingerie department picks up a nightgown. Elise says, "That nightgown comes in five different colors."

_____ 2. A customer in the electronics department wants to look at a small radio. Elise says, "Why don't you hold it? I'll show you how the electronic dial works."

_____ 3. A customer stops to look at a shirt. Elise watches the customer, but she does not say anything.

_____ 4. A customer in the women's department is carrying two dresses. Elise offers to hold the dresses until the customer is ready to try them on.

_____ 5. A customer wants to look at a handbag that is hanging on a wall behind the counter. Elise takes the handbag to the customer and talks about its features.

Listen and Speak

Step 1:   Listen as your teacher reads the conversation.

Elise: Those are pretty sweaters, aren't they?

Cherice: Yes. [*looks up*] Hi, Elise! Are you a saleswoman here?

Elise: Hi, Cherice. Yes, I work here part-time, after school and on weekends.

Cherice: How do you like working here? What do you do, anyway?

Elise: I like sales a lot. But I had to get used to doing lots of back-up work.

Cherice: Back-up work? What's that?

Elise: We sort, dust, straighten, and put garments on the racks. There's a lot to do to keep the department looking good. Are you looking for anything in particular?

Cherice: Yes. I'm looking for the ZaZoo jeans I saw in your ad. I don't see them. Do you have any left?

Elise: Those jeans are so popular that we just sold out. I can call some of our other stores to see if they have any. They can hold them or send them here for you.

Cherice: Thanks. I'd like that. I can pick them up at another store, if it's close. I wear a size nine.

Elise: Why don't you browse? Maybe you'll find something else you need.

   LATER

Elise: Cherice, they put aside a pair of jeans for you at our Five Streets Mall store. They're on a hold for a half day. Can you get there today?

Cherice: Yes, I think so. By the way, I want to try on these tops.

Elise: I'll start a dressing room for you. Then you can look around some more.

Cherice: You're really good at sales. I think I might like this kind of work, too.

Elise: They're hiring sales associates for the holidays now. Why don't you apply?

Step 2:   Read the conversation with another student.

Practice

Step 1: Fill in the missing words from the conversation on page 18.

Cherice: _____ do you like working here? _____ do

you _____, anyway?

Elise: I like sales a lot. But I had to get used to doing lots of _____

work.

Cherice: Back-up work? What's that?

Elise: We sort, _____, straighten, and put garments on the

_____. There's a lot to do to keep the _____

looking good. Are you _____ for anything in particular?

Cherice: Yes. I'm looking for the ZaZoo jeans I saw in your _____. I

don't_____ them. Do you have any _____?

Elise: Those jeans are so popular that we just _____

_____. I can call some of our other _____

to see if they have any. They can _____ them or

_____ them here for you.

Cherice: Thanks. I'd like that. I can _____ them _____

at another store, if it's close. I wear a _____ nine.

Step 2: Read each sentence. Write *Sales* in the space if the sentence tells about
selling. Write *Back-up work* if the sentence tells about some kind of
back-up work.

_____ **1.** I ask the customer how I can help.

_____ **2.** I dust the shelves.

_____ **3.** I take the clothes out of the dressing room and put them back
on the racks.

_____ **4.** I suggest that I can start a dressing room for the customer.

_____ **5.** I recommend trying this blouse with that skirt.

_____ **6.** I straighten the items on the shelves.

Be a Good Worker

Step 1: Listen as your teacher reads the information below. It is from a videotape for new workers at Davis and Landau.

A store is only as good as its sales staff. It's important for the sales staff to look professional. Our store, like most stores, has a strict dress code.

Dress Code for Davis and Landau Employees:
1. Wear shirts and blouses that are professional. No T-shirts or tank tops.
2. Wear slacks or tailored pants. No jeans.
3. Wear dress shoes. No tennis shoes, hiking or cowboy boots, or sandals.
4. Wear only a little jewelry.
5. Men must wear ties.
6. Women must wear skirts no shorter than knee length.
7. Women must wear stockings with skirts.
8. Women must wear only a little makeup.
9. Be friendly and wear a smile, too!

Step 2: Circle the pictures of workers who follow the dress code. With a partner, discuss the pictures you circled.

1.

2.

3.

4.

Have Some Fun!

Use the words in the list to complete the sentences below.
Place the answers in the puzzle.

anything	department	items	service
appliances	dust	merchandise	smile
customers	friendly	racks	special

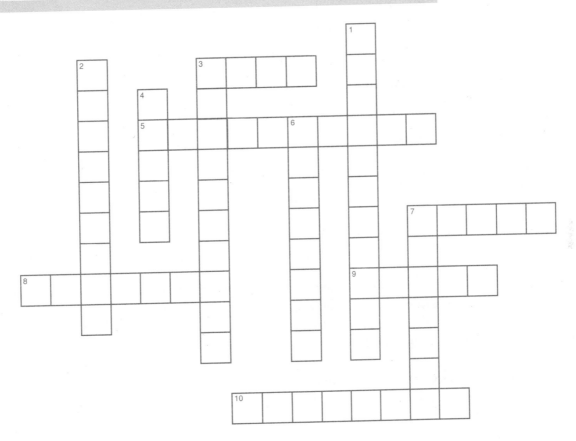

Across

3. I _____ the items on the shelves as my back-up work.

5. A curling iron and an electric knife are small _____.

7. Be friendly and wear a _____ on your face.

8. A salesperson must give good _____ to the customer.

9. The customers don't just want to buy _____. They want respect, too.

10. Always be _____ to customers.

Down

1. Stores sell _____.

2. We're here to serve _____.

3. Davis and Landau is a _____ store.

4. Stores hang clothes on _____.

6. "Are you looking for _____ special?"

7. "If you're looking for something _____, I can help you."

Think It Over

Step 1: Sometimes workers begin a sales conversation by talking about merchandise. Elise does this on page 18 when she says, "Those are pretty sweaters, aren't they?" This sales technique is called a merchandise approach. For each item below, write *Yes* if a merchandise approach is used. Write *No* if a merchandise approach is not used.

1. _____ Hello. How are you today?

2. _____ Those pants would look nice with your shirt.

3. _____ Those socks are very good for cold weather.

4. _____ That's a great buy on towels, isn't it?

5. _____ I can help the next person in line.

6. _____ That button is for the flash.

7. _____ Aren't those beautiful colors on those coats?

8. _____ There's no waiting on register three.

9. _____ That's the newest style in suits.

Step 2: A good salesperson asks open-ended questions to find out what customers need. Open-ended questions begin with *who, what, when, where, why,* or *how.* These questions do not have simple *yes* or *no* answers. Place a check mark next to the questions that are open ended.

_____ 1. How can I help you this evening?

_____ 2. May I help you?

_____ 3. Is this for yourself or for a gift?

_____ 4. What kind of shoes do you need?

_____ 5. Do you need a jacket?

_____ 6. Do you prefer this jacket or that one?

_____ 7. May I start a dressing room for you?

_____ 8. What style of pants do you like?

_____ 9. Which color do you prefer?

_____ 10. Would you like to try on that dress?

Check Your Understanding

Step 1: Circle *True* if the sentence is true and *False* if it is false.

1. If a customer says, "I'm just looking," say, "OK."	**True**	**False**
2. A good salesclerk suggests other products to go with a customer's selections.	**True**	**False**
3. If a customer picks up an item, that means she or he is not interested in it.	**True**	**False**
4. A salesperson should give a product to the customer to handle.	**True**	**False**
5. A salesclerk must do a lot of back-up work and give other workers a hand.	**True**	**False**
6. A good salesperson asks a lot of yes-or-no questions.	**True**	**False**
7. Sales associates do not have to listen to customers' answers.	**True**	**False**

Who Says It?

Step 2: Write *C* if a customer says it. Write *S* if a salesperson says it.

_____ 1. I want to browse a little.

_____ 2. I have time to do my back-up work.

_____ 3. No, thank you. I'm just looking.

_____ 4. Hello. How may I help you today?

_____ 5. I'd like to try these on.

_____ 6. I'll start a dressing room for you.

_____ 7. I can call our other store for you.

_____ 8. I'm looking for the shoes I saw in your ad.

_____ 9. Do you have shirts that go with these pants?

_____ 10. I can hold it for you.

Step 3: Place a check mark next to the sentences that show a good sales approach.

1. _____ Smile and make good eye contact.

2. _____ Do back-up work while customers wait.

3. _____ Ask open-ended questions.

4. _____ Be friendly.

5. _____ Never use a greeting approach.

6. _____ Use a merchandise approach.

Complete these activities.

1. Work with a small group of students. Discuss the following questions; and then write your answers to them.

   • Have you ever worked as a salesperson?

   • If so, what products or services did you sell?

   • What products or services would you like to sell?

2. Go to a local department store. Find the answers to the questions below. Share your answers with the class.

   • Do the salesclerks help the customers in the way they do in this unit?

   • Do sales associates also work as cashiers?

   • What kinds of sales approaches do you see?

   • Look at the store directory. Which departments in your local store are in Davis and Landau? Which departments are not in Davis and Landau?

3. Find out how much new salesclerks earn per hour at the stores near your home. Also find out if there are any benefits for workers at these department stores.

Notes

_____

_____

_____

_____

_____

_____

_____

_____

_____

_____

_____

_____

Unit 3
DO YOU HAVE AN ACCOUNT?

Look at the picture. Where are the people? What are they doing?
What do you think they are saying?

Words to Know

account	goal	(to) earn	major
application	incentive point	(to) fill out	plaid
article	percent	(to) initial	ready
blazer	sensor	(to) remove	voided
cashier	stamp	(to) ring up	wrong
check	trip	(to) talk into	
checking account	trouble	(to) void	It's not a problem.
choice			That's not a bad
discount	(to) cause	enough	idea.
driver's license	(to) change one's	instant	
garment bag	mind		

Listen and Speak

Step 1:   Listen as your teacher reads the conversation.

Sales Associate: Are you ready?

Customer: Yes. I decided on these two dresses.

Sales Associate: Good choice. Our cashier, Angie, will ring them up for you.

Angie: Who was helping you?

Customer: That nice saleswoman in the plaid blazer.

Angie: Will that be cash or charge?

Customer: I'd like to write a check.

Angie: Your total is sixty-eight dollars and forty-nine cents.

Customer: Do you have a stamp with the store name?

Angie: Yes, we do. Is this your correct address and phone number?

Customer: No, the phone number is wrong. It's 555-5582.

Angie: I'll need to see your driver's license and a major credit card.

Customer: Here you are. You know what? I only have enough money in my checking account for one item. I'll take this one. You can put this one back.

Angie: O.K. I'll void the sales receipt.

Customer: Oh, I'm sorry to cause you that trouble.

Angie: Don't worry. It's not a problem. So you have an Instant Account? Then you can charge both articles. It only takes a few minutes, and you get a 10-percent discount on everything you purchase today.

Customer: That's not a bad idea. Do you have an application to fill out?

Angie: Certainly. I'll remove the sensors from your dresses and get a garment bag.

LATER

Angie: Can you please initial this voided receipt? The customer changed her mind. But I talked her into opening an account. So she charged everything.

Manager: Good work. You earn incentive points for every new account. And you help your department reach its goal. Maybe you'll win the trip to Hawaii!

```
DAVIS AND LANDAU
.................
SALES RECEIPT    7/25
7217 Dress
7649 Dress         29.99
   Tax             32.99
Total               5.51
Check              68.49
#351               68.49
Change
                     .00
Thank You
```

Step 2:   Read the conversation in a small group. Then answer these questions:
   • Why did Angie talk to the customer about opening a charge account?
   • Why did Angie have the manager initial the voided receipt?

Practice

Step 1: Draw a line from the beginning of the sentence on the left to the end on the right.

1. I'd like to write
2. Will that be
3. I'll need to see your
4. Is this your correct
5. Would you like to open
6. Can you please initial this

a. address and phone number?
b. driver's license and a major credit card.
c. cash or charge?
d. voided receipt?
e. a check.
f. an Instant Account?

Step 2: You are the cashier. Complete the conversation with a partner. Then practice the conversation.

You: Who was _____?

Customer: _____.

You: Will _____?

Customer: I'd like to write a check.

You: Your total is _____.

Customer: O.K.

You: Is this your _____?

Customer: Yes.

You: I'll need to see _____.

Customer: Here you are.

You: Thank you. Here's your receipt.

Customer: Thank you.

Build Your Vocabulary

Words to Know

amount tendered	dollar coin	signature	(to) postdate
attention	expiration date	slot	
bill	half dollar	supervisor	alert
cash drawer	identification	transaction	correct
coin	nickel	tray	fewest
counterfeit	orientation		proper
detection pen	penny	(to) expire	suspect
credit department	protection	(to) face	
dime	quarter	(to) make change	aloud
direction	register plate	(to) match	silently

Step 1:   Read what the manager says at the orientation meeting.

"There are three common types of sales transactions: check, charge, and cash. When a customer writes a check, be sure to ask for proper identification: a driver's license and a major credit card. Then look at the check closely.
- Does the check have the correct date? Never let a customer postdate a check.
- Does the signature match those on the credit card and driver's license?
- Is the address on the check the same as the address on the identification?
- Is the dollar amount on the check the same as the amount of the purchase?
- Is the phone number on the check correct? Ask the customer.

When a customer charges the purchase, look at the credit card.
- Check the expiration date. Has the card expired? If it has, send the customer to a service phone to call the credit department.
- Look at the signature on the back of the card. Does it match the customer's signature? If the card is not signed, ask the customer to sign it for protection.

When a customer gives you cash, be alert and pay attention as you make change.
- Put the money on the register plate, or hold it in your hand. Say, 'Out of (ten, twenty, fifty, etc.) dollars.' The money that you take from the customer is called the amount tendered.
- Count the change silently first. Then count it aloud to the customer, placing the money in his or her hand. Give the fewest coins possible in change.
- Use a counterfeit detection pen to mark all large bills. If the pen leaves a yellow mark, the bill is good. If the pen leaves a black mark, the bill is suspect. Show your supervisor.
- Store money in the cash drawer. One-dollar bills go in the far right slot, followed by five-dollar bills, ten-dollar bills, twenty-dollar bills, and checks. Larger bills go under the tray. All bills face the same direction. Coins start with pennies on the right, then nickels, dimes, and quarters. Half dollars and dollar coins go on the far left side of the cash drawer."

Step 2:   With a group of two or three students, review the important points for handling each type of transaction.

Practice

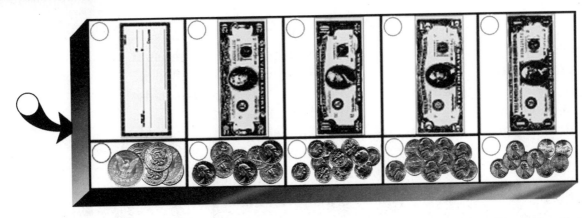

Step 1: Look at the cash drawer above. Fill in the circles with letters from the list below to show where the bills, coins, and checks go.

a. checks

b. dimes

c. ten-dollar bills

d. five-dollar bills

e. pennies

f. fifty- and one-hundred-dollar bills

g. twenty-dollar bills

h. nickels

i. one-dollar bills

j. quarters

k. half dollars and dollar coins

Step 2: Read each sentence. Does the sentence show a cash, check, or charge transaction? Write *cash*, *check*, or *charge* after each sentence.

1. "Is this your correct address and phone number?" _____

2. "I'll need to see your driver's license and a major credit card." _____

3. "That will be six dollars and five cents out of ten dollars." _____

4. "You need to sign the back of your card." _____

5. "Your card has expired. You have to call the credit department." _____

6. "Today's date is May 6. You have May 7." _____

7. "Yes, we have a stamp with the store name on it." _____

8. "Please sign the sales receipt." _____

9. "Your change is $10.05." _____

10. "You gave me a twenty. Here it is." _____

Listen and Speak

Words to Know

currency	scam	(to) replace	unusual
denomination	(a) ten	(to) sound like	after all
guy	victim		already
lost-and-found		distracted	
quick change artist	(to) balance	expensive	That comes to . . .
		short	

Step 1: Listen as your teacher reads the conversation.

Marvin: That comes to $5.14.

Customer 1: Here you are.

Marvin: Your change is $4.66. That's one, two, three, four, and sixty-six cents.

Customer 2: Excuse me. Where is the lost-and-found department?

Marvin: It's in the customer service department on the third floor.

Customer 1: [to Marvin] I gave you a twenty-dollar bill.

Marvin: Oh, you did? Well then, here's a ten.

LATER:

Marvin: Marco, I have to tell you something. I can't understand why my cash drawer is ten dollars short. I've counted and recounted, but it doesn't balance.

Marco: Think back, did anything unusual happen?

Marvin: Well, yes. Maybe that guy didn't give me a twenty-dollar bill after all.

Marco: It sounds like a scam. You may be the victim of a quick-change artist.

Marvin: How could that happen? Will I have to replace the money?

Marco: Probably. That's why you always have to be alert. Don't get distracted. Don't put the money the customer gives you in the cash drawer right away. Hold it or put it on the register plate. Then say the denomination of the bill aloud.

NEXT DAY:

Marvin: That will be $9.67 . [customer gives Marvin ten dollars] Out of ten dollars. Thirty-three cents is your change. Thank you, and come again.

Marco: You left the currency out until you finished the sale. You're learning fast.

Marvin: Yes, I am. I learned an expensive lesson already!

Step 2: Read the conversation with a partner or a small group. Then answer these questions:

- Why is it important to be alert when handling money?
- What did the quick-change artist do? When did Marvin find out?

Practice

Step 1: Write *T* on the line if the sentence is true. Write *F* if it is false.

_____ **1.** Marvin told Customer 1 the cost of the purchase.

_____ **2.** Marvin said aloud the denomination of the bill Customer 1 gave him.

_____ **3.** Customer 2 asked Marvin a question which distracted him.

_____ **4.** Marvin remembered how much money Customer 1 gave him.

_____ **5.** At first, Marvin couldn't understand why the money in his cash drawer did not balance.

_____ **6.** Marvin put the customer's money in the cash register too fast.

_____ **7.** Marvin may have to replace the extra money he gave the customer.

_____ **8.** Marvin said he learned a cheap lesson.

Step 2: Work with a partner. Answer the questions below.

1. Customer A bought a shirt for a total of $16.45. He gave the sales associate a twenty-dollar bill. How much was the change? _____

2. Customer B bought shoes for $33.22. The customer gave the sales associate a fifty-dollar bill. How much was the change? _____

3. Customer C bought a ring for $63.49. The customer gave the sales associate a hundred-dollar bill. How much was the change? _____

Step 3: With your partner, use the information from question 1, 2, or 3 in Step 2 to complete this conversation. Then practice with a partner.

Cashier: That comes to _____.

Customer: Here you are.

Cashier: Out of _____.

Customer: Yes.

Cashier: Your change is _____.

Customer: Thank you.

Cashier: You're welcome. Here's your receipt. Thank you for shopping at

_____.

Be a Good Worker

Step 1: **Work with a partner. Read the information below.**

A store cannot stay in business without customers. It is important for workers to give good customer service. An employee who gives good customer service follows these two rules:

  1. Do everything you can to find the merchandise your customers want.
  2. Treat customers well.

Step 2: **Can you give good customer service? Read each sentence below. Write *Yes* if the sentence is true for you. Write *No* if it is not.**

_____ **1.** I like to be around people.

_____ **2.** Smiling is easy for me. I smile often.

_____ **3.** I get along with people. People like to be with me.

_____ **4.** I like to be of service to others.

_____ **5.** I am able to follow rules and regulations.

_____ **6.** I can work quickly and accurately.

_____ **7.** It is easy for me to be nice to other people.

_____ **8.** I leave my personal life at home. I do not bring it to work.

_____ **9.** I am an honest person.

_____ **10.** I cooperate with others.

_____ **11.** I can pay close attention to what I am doing.

_____ **12.** I like to see people happy.

_____ **13.** I have a positive attitude.

_____ **14.** I know how to work as part of a team.

_____ **15.** I am a friendly person. I enjoy meeting new people.

Count your *Yes* and *No* answers. Write the number of answers below.

My Number of *Yes* answers: _____

My Number of *No* answers: _____

If you have almost all *Yes* answers, you will do well in a customer service job. If not, repeat this activity later. Think about the sentences. Try to make them true for you!

Have Some Fun!

Find the words from the box in the puzzle below. The words may be horizontal, vertical, or diagonal. They may even be backward. Circle the words you find.

account	check	expensive	sensor
alert	coin	expiration	signature
application	counterfeit	garment bag	slot
article	currency	orientation	transaction
bill	denomination	percent	tray
cash drawer	distracted	point	victim
cashier	discount	scam	

D	E	I	G	T	N	I	O	P	A	L	E	R	T	H	T	N
S	X	E	A	E	V	I	S	N	E	P	X	E	K	A	I	O
A	P	G	R	S	E	N	S	O	R	V	R	W	C	P	E	I
J	I	O	M	U	T	N	E	C	R	E	P	A	E	P	F	T
O	R	I	E	N	T	A	T	I	O	N	S	R	H	L	R	A
V	A	W	N	C	Z	A	B	T	M	Y	C	D	C	I	E	N
I	T	R	T	E	S	I	N	D	R	O	A	H	G	C	T	I
C	I	E	B	N	L	U	T	G	I	A	M	S	L	A	N	M
T	O	I	A	L	O	B	F	N	I	U	Y	A	Q	T	U	O
I	N	H	G	C	T	T	R	A	N	S	A	C	T	I	O	N
M	E	S	C	U	R	R	E	N	C	Y	B	K	A	O	C	E
P	K	A	S	C	H	F	X	D	I	S	C	O	U	N	T	D
E	L	C	I	T	R	A	D	I	S	T	R	A	C	T	E	D

Think It Over

Step 1:   Work with a partner. Read about handling money.

Handling money is an important part of every sales associate's job. The sales associate must be careful and always alert around money. Here are some things the sales associate must remember when handling money:

- Always close the cash drawer after each transaction.
- Never give back money if a customer says he or she gave you more money. Take the customer's name and phone number. Then you can call the customer if you have extra money when you balance your drawer at the end of the day.
- Count a customer's change silently first. Then count it aloud to the customer, placing it in his or her hand.
- Keep cash drawer organized with all of the bills facing one direction. You will see mistakes right away.

Step 2:   You are a sales associate. Read and discuss the questions below. Then write your answers on the lines below.

1. Why should you close the cash drawer after each transaction?

_____

_____

2. When a customer gives you money, should you put it in the cash drawer immediately? Explain your answer.

_____

_____

3. Why should the bills in the cash drawer face the same direction?

_____

_____

4. Why should you count a customer's change silently and then out loud?

_____

_____

5. If a customer says that you did not give him or her enough change, what should you do? Explain your answer.

_____

_____

Check Your Understanding

Circle the correct letter after each question.

1. If a customer writes a check, the salesperson must see the customer's
   a. driver's license and major credit card.
   b. charge account.
   c. checkbook.

2. A sales associate should make sure that the address and phone number on the customer's check are
   a. the same.
   b. correct.
   c. on the credit card.

3. In many stores, a sales associate gets an incentive when a customer
   a. uses a credit card.
   b. opens a checking account.
   c. opens a credit account.

4. The sales associate should be sure to give the customer
   a. a receipt.
   b. an account.
   c. a check.

5. What are the three types of sales transactions?
   a. cash drawer, cash register, change
   b. cash, check, charge
   c. charge account, checking account, savings account

6. A counterfeit detection pen can be used to find out
   a. the denomination of currency.
   b. if the currency is old.
   c. if the currency is good.

7. A quick-change artist
   a. wants change right away.
   b. tries to get more change from an employee.
   c. changes clothing fast.

8. A sales associate must always
   a. put customer's money in the cash drawer before giving change.
   b. get distracted.
   c. be alert.

9. Good customer service
   a. is not important in the retail business.
   b. can be learned.
   c. is not good for customers.

10. To give good service, a sales associate must
    a. know how to say "no."
    b. like to work alone.
    c. enjoy being of service to others.

11. A salesperson voids a sales receipt when
    a. the customer pays for a purchase.
    b. the customer changes the purchase.
    c. the customer pays with a credit card.

12. Where in a cash drawer do you put ten-dollar bills?
    a. under the tray.
    b. between the five-dollar bills and the twenty-dollar bills.
    c. between the pennies and the dimes.

Complete activity 1, 2, or 3 in class. Then do activities 4 and 5 on your own. Write your answers on the lines below or on another sheet of paper.

1. Work with a partner. Take turns being the customer and the salesperson. Role-play the following situations:
   - A sales transaction paid with a check
   - A sales transaction paid with cash
   - A sales transaction with a voided receipt
   - A sales transaction with a quick-change artist

2. Form a group of four or five students. Discuss the following questions:
   - Have you, or anyone you know, ever been the victim of a scam?
   - What are some of the scams you have heard about?
   - What are some things a salesperson can do to avoid scams?

3. If the cash in a cash drawer is short, the salesperson usually has to replace the missing amount. Do you think this rule is fair? Why? Discuss your answer with a partner. Then write a paragraph to explain your answer.

4. Imagine that you own a store. Describe the ideal worker you would have in your store.

5. Do you own any credit cards? What are the advantages and disadvantages of using credit cards? Make a list with two columns. In the first column, list the advantages of using credit cards. In the second column, list the disadvantages. Share you list with the class.

Notes

_____

_____

_____

_____

_____

_____

_____

_____

Unit 4
WOULD YOU LIKE SOMETHING ELSE?

Look at the picture. What do you think is happening? Who are the people?
What do you think they are saying?

Words to Know

commission	silk	(to) credit	nervous
copy	training	(to) enter	just
fabric	uneven exchange	(to) get in	perfectly
gift	wool	(to) go with	
gift wrapping	marked down	(to) return	over there
hanger			
mistake	(to) come first	long	Don't worry.
return	(to) convince	navy	

Listen and Speak

Step 1: Listen as your teacher reads the conversation.

Cherice: This is my first day. I'm a little nervous. I don't want to make a mistake.

Marco: Don't worry. You'll do fine. Smile and think, "Our customers come first."

LATER

Customer: Hi. I want to return this jacket. Here's my receipt.

Cherice: Would you like another size?

Customer: I don't think so. I don't like the fabric.

Cherice: Would you something else? We have some nice wool jackets just marked down on the rack over there. They're a great bargain.

Customer: Oh. Do you have a 42 long in navy?

Cherice: I'll check. [*walks to rack and finds a jacket*] Here's one. Would you like to try it on?

Customer: No, it's for a gift.

Cherice: How about a silk shirt to go with the jacket? We just got these in. The colors go perfectly with the jacket.

Customer: OK. You convinced me. Do you have this one in a large?

Cherice: Yes, we do. Will this be on your charge?

Customer: Yes. Here's my card.

Cherice: I'll credit your account first. Marco, how do I enter this on the register?

Marco: This is an uneven exchange. I'll show you what to do.

Cherice: [*to customer*] Here's your receipt, sir. Please sign on the line. I'll put your copy in the bag with your shirt. Would you like your jacket on the hanger?

Customer: Yes, please. Do you have gift wrapping?

Cherice: Yes, we do. The gift wrapping department is on the third floor in customer service. Thank you for shopping at Davis and Landau.

Customer: Thanks. [*customer leaves*]

Marco: That was good. You turned a return into a purchase and earned commission, too.

Cherice: I learned that in training. Thanks for your help.

Marco: No problem. We're a team here.

Step 2: Read the conversation with a group of three students.

Step 3: Answer these questions in your group:

- Why did Cherice ask the customer if he would like to look for something else?

- Why did Marco tell Cherice that what she did was good?

Practice

Step 1: Read the sentences below. Then circle *T* for true and *F* for false.

1. Cherice says it is her first day.	T	F
2. Marco says he is a little nervous.	T	F
3. The customer wants another size.	T	F
4. Cherice finds a new jacket for the customer.	T	F
5. The customer wants a navy jacket in size 42 long.	T	F
6. Cherice asks the customer if he would like a shirt to go with the jacket.	T	F
7. The customer tells Cherice that he wants a shirt to go with the jacket.	T	F
8. Cherice knows how to enter the sale into the cash register.	T	F
9. Cherice asks the customer to sign the receipt on the line.	T	F
10. Cherice puts the customer's receipt in the bag.	T	F

Step 2: Read the sentences. Write *C* on the line if the customer says it.
Write *S* on the line if the sales associate says it.

1. _____ "I want to return this shirt."

2. _____ "Would you like to look around for something else?"

3. _____ "Would you like to try it on?"

4. _____ "Here's my card."

5. _____ "Here's your receipt."

6. _____ "Do you have this in a medium?"

7. _____ "Please sign on the line."

8. _____ "I'll put your receipt in the bag."

9. _____ "Do you have gift wrapping?"

10. _____ "I'll credit your account."

Step 3: With a partner, role-play handling returns. Take turns being the customer and being the sales associate.

Build Your Vocabulary

Words to Know

action	(to) complain	mad
complaint	(to) deal with	pleasant
guideline	(to) enforce	polite
policy	(to) fix	rude
reason	(to) interrupt	sympathetic
tone	(to) repeat	
		calmly
(to) acknowledge	angry	
(to) apologize	difficult	

Step 1: Read what the store manager tells the sales associates to do when customers complain.

"Today you're going to learn about handling customer complaints. When customers are difficult to deal with, usually there's a reason. They're not mad at you. But it's your job to work with them. Always be polite to the customer, even if the customer is rude to you. Here are some guidelines to follow when a customer complains:

- Listen carefully. Give the customer your total attention. Use good eye contact and be sympathetic.

- Don't interrupt. Let the customer finish talking.

- Repeat what the customer says to be sure you understand his or her feelings. Speak calmly and use a pleasant tone of voice.

- Apologize and acknowledge the customer's situation.

- Say what you'll do to fix the situation.

Remember, the customer wants someone to handle the situation. As a sales associate, your job is to enforce store policy. If you can't resolve a customer's problem, call the floor manager. It'll be the manager's job to assist the customer and give the customer what he or she wants. Our customers come first. Nothing is more important. Without them, we wouldn't have jobs."

Step 2: With a partner, study the guidelines for handling a customer complaint. Try to name them without looking at the page.

Step 3: With your partner, talk about the guidelines. For each guideline, give one reason why it is important.

Practice

Step 1: Put a check mark next to a guideline for handling a customer complaint.

_____ 1. Listen carefully to what the customer says.

_____ 2. Interrupt the customer as often as you can.

_____ 3. Look at the floor and the ceiling at all times.

_____ 4. Repeat what the customer said to be sure you understand.

_____ 5. Use an angry tone of voice if the customer does.

_____ 6. Say what you will do to fix the situation.

_____ 7. Ask the customer to wait while you help other customers.

_____ 8. Tell the customer, "You're being difficult to deal with."

_____ 9. Be sympathetic to the customer's situation.

_____ 10. Say, "It's not my problem. Talk to someone else."

Step 2: On the left are guidelines for handling customer complaints. On the right are examples of what employees say to handle customer complaints. Draw lines to connect the guidelines with the correct examples.

1. Listen carefully.

2. Don't interrupt.

3. Repeat when the customer said.

4. Apologize.

5. Say what you will do to fix the situation.

a. "I'm sorry that you're unhappy with your purchase, Mrs. Green."

b. "So, you say you never received the merchandise you ordered?"

c. "I'll let you finish what you have to say."

d. "I'll call the manager right away. I'm sure he can resolve the problem."

e. "I can give you my total attention now."

Listen and Speak

Step 1: Listen as your teacher reads the conversation.

Customer: I want to return this coat. I'm in a hurry. I want my money back.

Cherice: Do you have your receipt?

Customer: Yes. Here it is. I bought the coat yesterday. It doesn't fit right.

Cherice: I see you paid by check. Our return policy is to wait ten days for your check to clear. Then we'll send you a check in the mail.

Customer: I don't want to wait. I want my money back now! I want a refund.

Cherice: I can understand that you want your money right away. I apologize for the inconvenience, but I have to follow store policy.

Customer: If I don't get my money now, I won't shop here ever again!

Cherice: I can understand that you're upset. I'm sorry, but I'm not authorized to give cash. I'll call the manager. I'm sure she'll be able to help you.

A FEW MINUTES LATER

Manager: Hello, ma'am. If you'll come with me to customer service, I'm sure we can resolve this situation to your satisfaction.

Customer: I sure hope so! [*manager and customer leave*]

Cherice: Wow! She was angry! What will happen next?

Alicia: Oh, the manager will give her what she wants. It's the manager's job to keep the customer satisfied. But you stayed calm. That was the correct thing to do.

Cherice: So, our job is to follow store policy.

Alicia: That's right. We do our job and the manager does her job.

Cherice: And the customer leaves happy.

Alicia: That's what it's all about!

Step 2: Read the conversation with a group of three students.

Step 3: Discuss these questions with your group:

- Was Cherice polite to the customer?
- Why does Cherice have to follow the store's return policy?

Practice

Draw a line from the beginning of each sentence to its correct ending.

1. Do you have

2. I apologize

3. I have to follow

4. I'm not authorized

5. I'm sure the manager

6. I'm sure we can resolve this situation

a. store policy.

b. will be able to fix the problem for you.

c. for the inconvenience.

d. to give you cash back.

e. your receipt?

f. to your satisfaction.

It's Your Turn

You are the salesperson. Complete the conversation below. Look at the conversation on page 42 if you need help. Then practice the conversation with a partner.

Customer: I want to return this _____. I'm in a _____.

I want _____.

You: _____.

Customer: Yes, I do. I bought _____.

You: I see you paid by _____. Our _____

is _____. Then we'll _____.

Customer: I don't want to wait. I want my money now.

You: I can understand _____. I'm sorry, but I'm not

_____. I'll call the _____. I'm sure

_____.

Be a Good Worker

Step 1: Listen as your teacher reads the information.

Good sales associates do not wait for customers to hand them something to buy. These sales associates think about how to expand a sale. Here are some things a good sales associate does to make or expand a sale:

1. Suggest other items for your customer to buy. Think of articles that go with what your customer has purchased. Show these items to your customer.

2. Find out why a customer is returning an item. Why does he or she want to return it? Turn the return into a sale by showing the customer what he or she wants.

3. Know what your customer likes. Call the customer when new merchandise arrives. Have the customer put his or her name on a mailing list. Then send the information.

4. Listen to your customers. Give your customer what he or she wants, and your sales will increase.

Step 2: Read the information with a partner.

Step 3: Circle the numbers of the sentences below that show what a salesperson can say to expand a sale.

1. "I'll credit your account with your return."

2. "Would you like to exchange the jacket for a different one? We just received some great new ones. Let me show you."

3. "This belt would look nice with your pants. The colors match perfectly."

4. "Will that be all?"

5. "Sorry, we don't have what you want."

6. "May I have your phone number, please? Then I can call you when we get the style you want."

7. "Sometimes we have sales."

8. "Would you like me to put your name on our mailing list? Then we can send you information about our special sales."

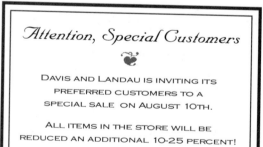

Attention, Special Customers

DAVIS AND LANDAU IS INVITING ITS PREFERRED CUSTOMERS TO A SPECIAL SALE ON AUGUST 10TH.

ALL ITEMS IN THE STORE WILL BE REDUCED AN ADDITIONAL 10-25 PERCENT!

STORE HOURS: 10 A.M. TO 7 P.M.

Have Some Fun!

Use the words in the box to complete the sentences below. Place the answers in the puzzle.

apologize	gift	resolve
bargain	mistake	return
calm	policy	wool
complaint		

Across

3. "I think we can _____ this situation."

4. Always listen carefully to a customer who has a _____.

5. Something you give to another person is a _____.

7. To say you are sorry is to _____.

8. Cherice does not want to make a _____.

Down

1. One fabric used to make jackets is _____.

2. A sales associate has to follow store _____.

3. To bring something back is to _____ it.

4. It is important to stay _____ when talking to an angry customer.

6. Something for sale at a very low price is a _____.

Think It Over

When a customer is mad, angry, or rude, there usually is a reason.
Put a check mark next to the reasons that show why a customer may
be difficult.

The customer:

_____ **1.** is in a bad mood.

_____ **2.** has problems at home or work.

_____ **3.** is sick, tired, or hungry.

_____ **4.** had a bad day.

_____ **5.** does not like the clothes the salesperson is wearing.

_____ **6.** is in a hurry and has been waiting a long time.

_____ **7.** is angry with his or her children or spouse.

_____ **8.** thinks the salesperson is not friendly.

_____ **9.** is upset about the merchandise he or she bought.

_____ **10.** is unhappy with the store's policy.

_____ **11.** was waiting longer than someone who was served first.

_____ **12.** does not like the salesperson's smile.

_____ **13.** had an argument with someone earlier.

_____ **14.** does not like shopping.

_____ **15.** thinks the salesperson's hair is too short.

_____ **16.** can not find what he or she wants.

What are some other reasons why a customer may be difficult?
Think of your own experiences as a customer. Write your reasons on
the lines below.

_____

_____

_____

_____

_____

_____

Check Your Understanding

Step 1: Imagine you are a sales associate. Circle the letter that shows the best way to finish each sentence.

1. If a customer is angry, you should
   a. help other customers.
   b. call the manager right away.
   c. give the customer your full attention and listen until he or she finishes talking.

2. If a customer tells you a problem, you should
   a. ask a co-worker to help the customer.
   b. help the customer to resolve the problem.
   c. leave for a break.

3. It is the sales associate's job to
   a. follow store policy and explain the policy to the customers.
   b. forget about store policy when he or she wants.
   c. be rude to customers who are rude.

4. When explaining store policy to customers, the sales associate should
   a. always be polite.
   b. never be polite.
   c. be polite sometimes and not polite sometimes.

Step 2: Circle the items that show what a sales associate should do when handling a customer complaint.

1. Listen carefully to the customer.

2. Repeat what the customer says to show understanding.

3. Interrupt the customer.

4. Apologize.

5. Help other customers first.

6. Tell the customer what you will do to help resolve the situation.

7. Speak in an angry tone of voice.

8. Tell the customer to go to another store.

Step 3: With a partner, practice role-playing how to handle the customer complaints below. Take turns being the customer and the sales associate.

1. "I want my money back for this electric knife!"

2. "I bought this jacket last week, and the zipper is broken!"

3. "This TV set doesn't work!"

Complete activity 1 or 2 in class. Then do activity 3, 4, or 5 on your own. Write your answers on the lines below or on another sheet of paper.

1. Why do customers return merchandise? Discuss this question with a partner. Make a list of reasons.

2. Many stores have a "no questions asked" return policy. Other stores ask the customer to fill out a form to explain why he or she is returning an item. Which policy do you think is best? Why? Discuss your answers with a partner.

3. Have you ever returned merchandise to a store? If so, why? Was the sales associate polite? What questions did he or she ask you? Write a paragraph that tells about your experience.

4. Go to three stores in your area and find out the return policy for each store. Answer the following questions:
   • How are the return policies similar? How are they different?
   • Are there different policies for different merchandise (for example, clothing and electronics)?

5. Talk to someone who works in a store. What ideas can this person give you about handling angry or rude customers?

Notes

_____

_____

_____

_____

_____

_____

_____

_____

_____

_____

_____

_____

Look at the picture. What is happening? What are the people doing?
What kind of store is pictured?

Words to Know

alarm	packages	(to) catch	latest
assistant manager	parking lot	(to) close (out)	
bank	patience	(to) escort	as a matter of fact
closing time	safe	(to) forget (forgot)	come again
code	security guard	(to) lock up	from time to time
cooperation	shoplifter	(to) prosecute	fullest extent of
deposit	sporting goods	(to) set	the law
electronic security	undercover security	(to) set off	Hey!
device	officer	(to) steal	
gate		(to) take care of	
inconvenience	(to) appreciate	(to) take off	
key	(to) apprehend		
mall	(to) be in charge		

Listen and Speak

Step 1: Listen as your teacher reads the conversations below. David and Irma work at Trout's Sporting Goods. Tony is their manager.

David: [*to customer*] You have a lot of packages, Mrs. Sanchez. Would you like me to call a mall security guard to escort you to your car?

Mrs. Sanchez: Yes, please. I would appreciate that. Last time, a guard helped me when my car wouldn't start in the parking lot.

LATER

Tony: Irma, I have to go to the bank to make a deposit. You and David are in charge. I won't be here tonight to lock up. I'll show you how to close the store.

Irma: OK, Tony. Don't worry. We'll take care of everything. [*alarm sounds*]

David: Uh-oh! Someone set off the alarm. It must have been that customer. I'll catch him. [*runs after man who just left the store*] Excuse me, sir. I think we forgot to take the sensor off your purchase. Please return to the store, so we can remove the device. Thank you for your cooperation.

Customer: Hey, I paid for this. Here's my receipt.

David: No problem. I'm sorry for the inconvenience. It was our mistake.

Customer: I understand. Do you catch many shoplifters?

David: Our undercover security officers apprehend them from time to time. We prosecute shoplifters to the fullest extent of the law.

Customer: That's good. How do you catch someone stealing?

David: We have the latest electronic security devices. There, I removed the sensor. Thanks for your patience. Come again to Trout's Sporting Goods.

LATER

David: Irma, who's going to set the alarm tonight? It's almost closing time, and Tony isn't here. I don't know the code, do you?

Irma: As a matter of fact, I do. Tony gave me the key to lock the gate. He also showed me how to close out the registers and put the money in the safe.

David: Hey! Maybe you'll be our next assistant manager!

Step 2: Read the conversations with a partner.

Step 3: Discuss these questions with your partner:
- Why did the customer show his receipt to David?
- Why do stores need to apprehend shoplifters?

Practice

Step 1: Match the beginning of each sentence on the left with its ending on the right. Write the letter of the correct ending on the line.

_____ 1. Thank you for your

_____ 2. Thank you for your

_____ 3. I'm sorry for the

_____ 4. It's almost

_____ 5. Our undercover security officers apprehend

_____ 6. We forgot to take off the

_____ 7. I have to go to the bank to make a

_____ 8. I know the code to set the

_____ 9. We prosecute shoplifters to the fullest extent of the

_____ 10. It was our

_____ 11. Please return to the

_____ 12. We have all of the latest

_____ 13. I have the key to lock the

_____ 14. I know how to put the money in the

_____ 15. Maybe you'll be our next

a. closing time.

b. law.

c. deposit.

d. gate.

e. store.

f. cooperation.

g. patience.

h. safe.

i. alarm.

j. assistant manager.

k. security devices.

l. sensor.

m. mistake.

n. inconvenience.

o. shoplifters.

Step 2: You are a sales associate. A customer just walked out of the store with an item, and you forgot to remove the sensor. What do you say? Work with a partner to complete the conversation below. Then practice the conversation with your partner.

1. **You:** Excuse me. Please _____.

   We forgot to _____.

2. **Customer:** OK. I have my receipt right here.

3. **You:** I'm sorry for the _____.

4. **Customer:** Do you catch many shoplifters?

5. **You:** _____.

6. **Customer:** That's good.

7. **You:** Thank you for _____.

Build Your Vocabulary

Words to Know

count	loss prevention	warning	
extension	markdown		accurate
floor	markup	(to) cause	dishonest
harm	operative	(to) control	external
high-ticket item	paperwork	(to) dial	internal
ink	profit	(to) log	permanent
ink sensor	responsibility	(to) page	personal
intercom	retail industry	(to) ruin	suspicious
inventory	tag	(to) shoot out	
layaway	theft	(to) split	"grab and run"
loss(es)	thief	(to) switch	

Step 1: The store manager is telling new employees about loss prevention. Read what the manager says.

"Loss prevention is very important in the retail industry. We have to control our losses, or we will not make a profit. Loss prevention is the responsibility of every retail employee. Here are some important points to remember:

- Be careful with your paperwork. Log markdowns and markups correctly.
- In the layaway department, always return expired layaways to the floor.
- Watch for internal (worker) and external (customer) theft. Call a loss prevention operative immediately if you see something suspicious.
- Know the prices of our merchandise. Sometimes dishonest customers switch tags. Always be alert.
- Be careful when you take inventory. We need an accurate count.
- Always remove sensors when you make a sale. We put sensors on all of our high-ticket items. We use special ink sensors on our grab and run items. If a thief tries to remove an ink sensor, it splits open and shoots out ink that ruins the garment. These sensors come with a warning because the ink is permanent and could cause personal harm.
- If you want to call a loss-prevention operative to your department, page Mr. Johnson on the intercom and say your telephone extension. This is the code we use. Someone will come right away.
- Remember, loss prevention is everyone's business."

WARNING
DO NOT TAMPER WITH
INK-MARK
PERMANENT INK CAN
RUIN GARMENT AND
CAUSE SERIOUS
PERSONAL
INJURY

Step 2: Read the story with a partner. Then answer these questions:

- Why is loss prevention important?
- What can an employee do to help with loss prevention?

Practice

Step 1: Use the words from the story on page 52 to fill in the spaces below.

1. Loss prevention is the _____ of every retail employee.

2. Be careful with your _____. A lot of loss is on paper.

3. Always return expired _____ to the floor.

4. Watch for internal and external _____. Call a _____
   _____ _____ if you see something suspicious.

5. Know the _____ of the merchandise. Sometimes dishonest customers
   switch _____. Always be _____.

6. Be careful when you take _____. We need an accurate
   _____.

7. We put _____ on all of our high-ticket items.

8. If a thief tries to remove an _____ _____, it splits
   open and shoots out _____.

9. Ink sensors come with a _____ because the ink is permanent and
   could cause personal harm.

10. _____ _____ is everyone's business.

Step 2: Work with a partner. Read each sentence below. Decide if the loss is an
external, an internal, or a paper loss. On the lines write *E* for external,
I for internal, and *P* for paper.

_____ 1. A shoplifter steals a jacket.

_____ 2. An employee takes money from the cash register.

_____ 3. A customer does not pick up a layaway. The garment is not returned
to the floor.

_____ 4. An employee takes a dress out of the store without paying for it.

_____ 5. A jacket is marked down from $39.99 to $24.99. Nothing is written in the
markdown log.

_____ 6. During an inventory, an employee forgets to count a rack of pants.

_____ 7. A customer switches tags and puts a lower price on an item. The employee
sells it for the lower price.

Listen and Speak

Words to Know

base	videotape		top
bracelet	watch	aware	
entrance		east	I'll be right with
evidence	(to) agree	lost	you.
gift certificate	(to) approach	lovely	in progress
parents	(to) pick (someone)	observant	Money-back
pocket	up	preoccupied	guarantee
robbery	(to) proceed	recorded	You're absolutely
timepiece	(to) watch	stupid	right.

Step 1: Listen as your teacher reads the conversation.

Customer 1: I found this little girl in the mall. She's lost.

Lisa: I'll call mall security to pick her up. Don't worry, we'll find her parents.

Customer 2: Excuse me. I'd like to see the watch on the top shelf.

Alex: Certainly, ma'am. Let me open the case. Here, put it on. It's a lovely timepiece. It comes with a guarantee. If you decide to return it, we'll refund your money. Also, all of our watches are 25 percent off this week.

Customer: I'll take it. I have a gift certificate.

LATER

Officer: I'm here for the lost child.

Lisa: She's right here.

Radio Voice: Base to security. Proceed to east entrance. Robbery in progress.

Officer: I have to go. I'll come back as soon as I can.

Lisa: Don't worry. We'll take good care of the little girl.

LATER

Lisa: Alex, I saw that woman put a bracelet in her pocket. What should I do?

Alex: Don't say anything. We need to get an undercover operative here to watch her. Page Mr. Smith on the intercom and give our phone extension.

Lisa: What will happen?

Alex: They won't do anything until she leaves the store. Then they'll approach her. They'll have evidence. Her actions were recorded on videotape.

Lisa: That was stupid of her. She could ruin her life.

Alex: You're absolutely right. I agree.

Step 2: Read the conversation with a group of three or four students.

Step 1: Write *T* in front of the sentence if it is true. Write *F* it is false.

_____ 1. Lisa found a lost little girl in the mall.

_____ 2. A customer asks Alex to see a watch in the case.

_____ 3. Alex tells the customer the watches were on sale last week.

_____ 4. Alex sells the watch to the customer.

_____ 5. Customer 2 charges her purchase.

_____ 6. The mother comes to pick up the lost child.

_____ 7. The mall security officer gets a call on his radio.

_____ 8. Lisa sees a customer put a bracelet in her pocket.

_____ 9. Alex tells Lisa to say something to the woman.

_____ 10. Alex says they need an undercover operative.

_____ 11. The operative will approach the woman before she leaves the store.

_____ 12. The woman's actions were recorded on videotape.

_____ 13. Lisa and Alex think the woman did a smart thing.

_____ 14. Lisa and Alex think the woman did a stupid thing.

Step 2: Next to each sentence below, write *C* if a customer would say it. Write *S* if a sales associate would say it.

_____ 1. "Excuse me. I want to see the watch on the top shelf."

_____ 2. "Let me open the case."

_____ 3. "All of our watches are on sale this week."

_____ 4. "It comes with a money-back guarantee."

_____ 5. "Here, put it on. It's a lovely timepiece."

_____ 6. "I'll take it."

_____ 7. "I have a gift certificate to use."

_____ 8. "I'll call mall security."

Be a Good Worker

Step 1: **Read about being a good listener.**

A good customer service worker is a good listener. To be a good listener, pay close attention to what the customer says. Do not think about other things. Turn your body toward the customer. Look at the customer. These things tell the customer that he or she is important.

Step 2: **Are you a good listener? Do you have good listening habits? Put a check mark next to the sentence if it is true for you.**

_____ 1. I look at the person who is speaking.

_____ 2. I give my total attention to what the speaker is saying.

_____ 3. I am patient. I allow lots of time to listen.

_____ 4. I turn my body toward the person who is speaking.

_____ 5. I nod my head to say "yes" or say things like "I see" to show that I am paying attention.

_____ 6. I think about the other person's feelings.

_____ 7. I listen to the speaker's tone of voice.

_____ 8. I study the speaker's body language, how he or she is moving.

_____ 9. I repeat what I think the other person said. I ask questions, so I will understand.

_____ 10. I do not interrupt. I let the person finish talking.

_____ 11. I do not finish the person's sentences.

_____ 12. I do not let other people interrupt us.

_____ 13. I do not get distracted by other things I need to do.

_____ 14. I do not think about what I will say next when the other person is talking.

_____ 15. I do not make judgments.

_____ 16. I do not make up my mind until I have all the information.

Step 3: **Count your check marks. Write the number below.**

My number of good listening habits: _____

You can learn to be a good listener! Practice listening to people. Keep working on this list until you can put a check mark next to every sentence.

Have Some Fun!

Find the words from the box below in the puzzle. The words may be horizontal, vertical, or diagonal. They may even be backward. Circle the words you find.

alarm	gate	loss prevention	security
code	internal	operative	suspicious
closing time	inventory	profit	tag
deposit	inconvenience	prosecute	theft
dishonest	ink sensor	remove	thief
evidence	law	responsibility	warning
external	layaway	safe	

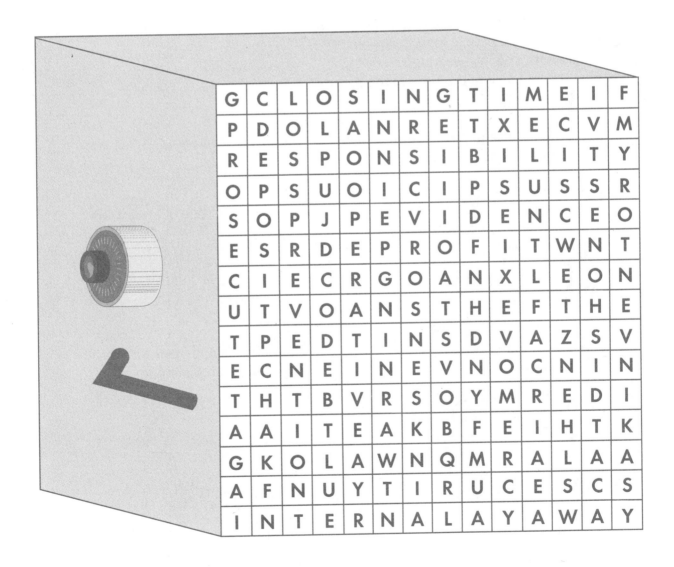

G	C	L	O	S	I	N	G	T	I	M	E	I	F
P	D	O	L	A	N	R	E	T	X	E	C	V	M
R	E	S	P	O	N	S	I	B	I	L	I	T	Y
O	P	S	U	O	I	C	I	P	S	U	S	S	R
S	O	P	J	P	E	V	I	D	E	N	C	E	O
E	S	R	D	E	P	R	O	F	I	T	W	N	T
C	I	E	C	R	G	O	A	N	X	L	E	O	N
U	T	V	O	A	N	S	T	H	E	F	T	H	E
T	P	E	D	T	I	N	S	D	V	A	Z	S	V
E	C	N	E	I	N	E	V	N	O	C	N	I	N
T	H	T	B	V	R	S	O	Y	M	R	E	D	I
A	A	I	T	E	A	K	B	F	E	I	H	T	K
G	K	O	L	A	W	N	Q	M	R	A	L	A	A
A	F	N	U	Y	T	I	R	U	C	E	S	C	S
I	N	T	E	R	N	A	L	A	Y	A	W	A	Y

Think It Over

Step 1: Read about being an observant worker.

Retail workers need to be observant. They must see and hear everything around them. They have to be aware, and they have to remember. Observant workers are always thinking about what other people are doing and saying. They are not preoccupied or busy thinking their own thoughts. When they are at work, they do not think about their personal lives or problems.

An observant worker makes customers feel important. An observant worker also notices anything that is suspicious or unusual.

Step 2: How observant are you? Work with a partner. Look at the picture on page 49 for ten seconds. Then try to answer these questions:

- What do you think is happening in the picture?
- How old do the people look?
- What are the people wearing?
- What is the name of the store in the picture?

Step 3: Look at the pictures below. Circle the picture that shows an observant worker.

1.

Tina is talking to her boyfriend on the phone.

3.

Mario is making plans for the weekend with his friends.

2.

John is giving his total attention to the customer.

4.

Sara is thinking about the test she has to take tomorrow.

Check Your Understanding

Circle the letter of the correct answer.

1. If an employee sells an item and forgets to remove the sensor,
   a. it is not a problem.
   b. the sensor will set off the alarm when the customer leaves the store.
   c. the customer will be happy.

2. Loss prevention is
   a. the responsibility of the store manager.
   b. the responsibility of every employee in the retail business.
   c. not important in the retail business.

3. Mall security officers
   a. never talk to customers.
   b. set off alarms.
   c. help customers and employees.

4. An inventory should always be
   a. accurate.
   b. done quickly.
   c. done by loss-prevention operatives.

5. At closing time, employees should
   a. leave right away.
   b. set off the store alarm.
   c. set the store alarm.

6. Sales associates should
   a. always be careful with paperwork.
   b. not return expired layaways to the floor.
   c. not log markdowns.

7. If a sales associate sees something suspicious, he or she should
   a. apprehend the person responsible.
   b. forget about it.
   c. call a loss-prevention operative.

8. Loss-prevention operatives can use videotaped recordings
   a. as evidence of shoplifting.
   b. to help find lost children.
   c. for sales associates to watch on break.

9. To catch shoplifters, stores use
   a. keys.
   b. electronic security devices.
   c. money.

10. Loss-prevention operatives look for
    a. internal and external theft and paper loss.
    b. high-ticket items.
    c. mall security.

11. Some stores keep high-ticket items in locked glass cases,
    a. so customers will not buy them.
    b. so they look nice.
    c. so they can stop shoplifters.

12. To be a good listener, a worker should
    a. not look at the speaker while he or she is talking.
    b. help the speaker by finishing his or her sentences.
    c. pay close attention to what the speaker is saying.

13. By being a good listener, a worker is telling the customer,
    a. "I want to give you my advice."
    b. "You are important to me."
    c. "You are not important to me."

14. Being observant means
    a. seeing and hearing everything that is happening around you.
    b. being preoccupied with your own thoughts.
    c. telling other people what you think.

Try It!

Complete activities 1, 2, and 3 in class. Then do activity 4 or 5 on your own. You can write on the lines below or on another sheet of paper.

1. Work with a partner. Discuss the questions below and then write your answers.
   - What is loss prevention? Why is it important?
   - What do loss-prevention operatives do?
   - Why is an accurate inventory important?

2. What makes a good listener? With a partner, write as many good listening habits as you can. Then practice being a good listener. Take turns speaking for a minute about what you did yesterday. Your partner should listen and then repeat the information to you.

3. Would you like to work in security or loss prevention? Make a list of reasons to explain your answer.

4. Practice being observant. Listen to someone talk for two or three minutes. The person can be someone on TV, a person you just met, or someone you already know. Try to write what each person looks like and what each person does and says. Keep practicing every time you talk with people at school and in the community.

5. Go to a mall and talk to the mall security officers. Ask them to describe their work. Do they do some of the jobs described in the unit? Report to the class about what you learned.

Notes

_____

_____

_____

_____

_____

_____

_____

_____

_____

What kinds of workers are in this picture? What do you think they are talking about?

Words to Know

A-frame rack	rolling rack	(to) be ready	in front of
arm (of a rack)	rounder	(to) bring	in the back
computer printout	sale item	(to) grab	in the middle
display department	sales floor	(to) move	make a big splash
four-way rack	side	(to) separate	next to
mannequin	stock	(to) size	on the left
placement	stock clerk		on the right
price tag	T-stand	clearance	
	vendor	early	
	waterfall rack		

Listen and Speak

Step 1: Listen as your teacher reads the conversation. Marisa is a sales manager at Davis and Landau. Joseph works in the display department. They and other workers are preparing the store for a sale.

Marisa: Good morning everyone. Our Pre-Inventory Sale starts in four hours. We want to make a big splash! This is Joseph from the display department. He'll show the stock clerks where to put racks and merchandise. Salesclerks, come with me.

Joseph: Last year's sale was great, but this one will be better! Let's put three rounders in the back of the sales floor and two A-frame racks in the middle.

Pat: OK. Carlo, grab one side, will you?

Carlo: Sure. Joseph, do you want us to set up mannequins, too?

Joseph: No, not this time. But we do need four waterfall racks on the walls and three four-way racks in front.

Pat: [*Points*] Shall we put the waterfalls up there, next to the shelves on the wall?

Joseph: Yes, that's good placement. After you do that, bring out the stock on the rolling racks in the back, OK?

MEANWHILE

Marisa: Every sale rack needs a sale sign. Also, clearance items should go on the rounders in the back, three sizes to a rounder. Stock clerks will help you move everything.

Jeff: Which are the "clearance" items and which are "sale" items?

Marisa: Clearance items are on this computer printout. [*hands Jeff and Natalie a printout*] All sale items have red price tags. Natalie, please size the markdown items from smallest to largest. Then put them on the A-frames with the smallest sizes in front, OK?

Natalie: Sure. Would you like me to separate them by vendor, too?

Marisa: Not the markdowns, but we do need to separate the new items on the four-ways and the T-stands by vendor. We want only one vendor per arm.

Natalie: OK, Marisa, I'll do that next.

Marisa: Jeff, separate the waterfalls by vendor and by color, too. Let's put blue clothes on this waterfall rack. Our blue Suzi Fong merchandise can go on the left, James Berg on the right, and Hot Image in the middle.

Jeff: Sure, Marisa, I'll sort them right now.

LATER

Marisa: Well, Joseph, the department looks great! We're ready for business.

Joseph: Yes, our people did a good job. Nice working with you. See you later.

Step 2: Read the conversation with a partner.

Practice

Step 1:   Draw a line to match the beginning of each sentence with its ending. If you need help, read the conversation on page 62 again.

1. Put the clearance items on rounders
2. The markdown items should go
3. New items go
4. The waterfall racks go on the walls,

a. on four-way racks in the front of the display area.
b. next to the shelves.
c. in the back of the display area.
d. on A-frame racks in the middle of the display area.

Step 2:   Display racks are named for what they look like. Work with a partner. Write the name of the rack under each picture below.

A-frame	rounder
four-way	T-stand
rolling rack	waterfall

1.

2.

3.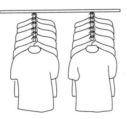

4.

5.

6.

Build Your Vocabulary

Words to Know

box cutter	shipment	(to) unload	soft
carton	stockroom	(to) unwrap	specific
contents	truck		
dollar amount	type	hard	
goods		hidden	
location	(to) make sure	high-priced	
receiving area	(to) process	high-theft	

Step 1: Read about Mitch's job.

Mitch is a processor for a department store. He works in the receiving area, where trucks bring new goods. He also works in the stockroom. When a truck comes in, sometimes Mitch helps the stock clerk unload it.

Mitch separates the shipment, counts the cartons, and checks in the new goods. He uses a box cutter to open the cases and unwraps any goods in plastic bags. He makes sure the contents of the cartons are correct. He puts sensors on goods that cost more than a certain dollar amount. He puts on soft or hard sensors, depending on the type of merchandise. He puts hidden sensors on high-priced items. Some high-theft items need two sensors, so he puts on two. He puts garments on the correct hangers.

Sometimes Mitch finds a carton that does not have what is supposed to be inside. Then he calls Loss Prevention. Sometimes he takes soft goods from the stockroom to the sales floor. All of the things Mitch does are called processing. He likes his job because he has a lot of variety and responsibility at work.

Step 2: Work with a partner. Discuss the following questions:

- What does Mitch do? Make a list of responsibilities.
- Do you like to have a lot of responsibility at work? Why?

Practice

Step 1:   Fill in the spaces with words from the story.

Mitch _____ the shipment, counts the _____,

and checks in the new goods. He uses a _____ to open the cases

and _____ any goods in plastic bags. He makes sure the contents of

the cartons are _____. He puts _____

on goods that cost more than a certain _____ amount. He puts on soft

or _____ sensors, depending on the type of _____.

He puts hidden sensors on _____ items. Some _____

items need two sensors, so he puts on two. He puts garments on the correct

_____.

Step 2:   Read each sentence. Circle *T* if the sentence is true and *F* if it is false.

1. Mitch works in the sales department.	T	F
2. He separates the hard sensors and soft sensors.	T	F
3. Sometimes Mitch unloads trucks.	T	F
4. Mitch does not put sensors on the goods that cost more than a certain amount.	T	F
5. He works with the stock clerks.	T	F
6. Mitch makes sure the contents of the cartons are correct.	T	F
7. Sometimes he calls Loss Prevention.	T	F

Listen and Speak

Words to Know

bin	hand truck	trailer	(to) lose
boss	load	trash	(to) recycle
bunch	metal	video	(to) stack
cardboard	pallet	wood	
cement	pallet jack		easy
compactor	paper	(to) avoid	empty
crack	plastic	(to) find out	tricky
crystal	towel	(to) get rid of	valuable

Step 1: Listen as your teacher reads the conversation.

Mitch: Are you the new stock clerk? The boss told you what to do, right?

Sal: Yes. He told me you'd help me out. He said that we're a team.

Mitch: That's right. I'm glad to help. Right now we're going to unload that trailer. I've got my hand truck. Have you got your pallet jack?

Sal: Got it. Should I take an empty pallet into the trailer with me?

Mitch: Go check. The boxes may already be on pallets in the truck. If not, take one up.

Sal: Where do I take this pallet of boxes?

Mitch: Take it over there for me to start processing. Be careful. Avoid cracks in the cement. You don't want to lose that load.

Sal: I'm glad I saw the video on stacking boxes. This isn't easy.

Mitch: Right. It's tricky to stack on the hand truck, too. I have to start processing this shipment now. Keep on emptying. Then you have to get rid of all the trash.

LATER

Mitch: You're almost finished. Good! Next, you'll need to sort all the packing material. [*pointing*] The cardboard goes into that compactor and then on that stack. Put the box cutter in the safety position when you finish so you don't cut yourself.

Sal: I will. Then I put this plastic, wood, metal, and paper in their recycling bins.

Mitch: Right. Hey, look. This box says "crystal" on it, but it's a bunch of towels.

Sal: Isn't Loss Prevention supposed to hear about this?

Mitch: Yeah. They'll find out what happened to the crystal. It's valuable. Well, these hard goods have sensors and are ready for you to take to the stockroom. I'll take the soft goods. If you don't know where to put things, I'll show you.

Sal: Thanks.

Step 2: Read the conversation with a partner.

Practice

Draw a line from the picture to the correct sentence.

1.

2.

3.

4.

5.

6.

7.

8.

a. Right now we're going to unload that trailer.

b. Have you got your pallet jack?

c. Should I take an empty pallet into the trailer with me?

d. Sometimes the boxes are already on pallets in the truck.

e. It's tricky to stack on the hand truck, too.

f. The cardboard goes into that compactor and then on that stack.

g. Put the box cutter in the safety position when you finish so you don't cut yourself.

h. Then I put this plastic, wood, metal, and paper in their recycling bins.

Be a Good Worker

Listen as your teacher reads the conversation. Marisa is a sales manager at Davis and Landau. Joseph works in the display department. They and other workers are preparing the store for a sale.

Marisa: Good morning everyone. Our Pre-Inventory Sale starts in four hours. We want to make a big splash! This is Joseph from the display department. He'll show the stock clerks where to put racks and merchandise. Salesclerks, come with me.

Joseph: Last year's sale was great, but this one will be better! Let's put three rounders in the back of the sales floor and two A-frame racks in the middle.

Pat: OK. Carlo, grab one side, will you?

Carlo: Sure. Joseph, do you want us to set up mannequins, too?

Joseph: No, not this time. But we do need four waterfall racks on the walls and three four-way racks in front.

Pat: [*Points*] Shall we put the waterfalls up there, next to the shelves on the wall?

Have Some Fun!

Use the words in the box to complete the sentences below. Place the answers in the puzzle.

Words to Know

arm	display	stack
box	hand truck	sensor
box cutter	pallet	stock clerk
carton	processor	vendor
case	rack	

Across

5. The _____ puts hard, soft, and hidden sensors on goods.

6. A _____ is about the same as a carton or box.

7. A "four-way" or a "rounder" is a kind of _____.

9. Be careful to _____ smaller cases on top of larger ones.

11. Never stack cases over the height of the top bar of a _____. It's too hard to balance.

12. A _____ is about the same as a carton or a case.

14. We want only one _____ per arm of the four-way rack.

Down

1. The _____ and the processor unloaded the truck and took the merchandise.

2. The _____ department got the store looking good for the big sale.

3. Sometimes the boxes are on a _____ on the truck.

4. Be careful to put your_____ in the safety position when you finish so you don't cut yourself.

8. Does this pair of shoes have a hidden _____ on it yet?

10. A _____ is about the same as a case or a box.

13. We want only one vendor per _____ of the four-way rack.

Think It Over

Step 1: What is wrong with each picture below? Write your answer on the lines below.

1.

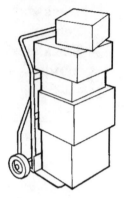

_____

_____

_____

3.

_____

_____

_____

2.

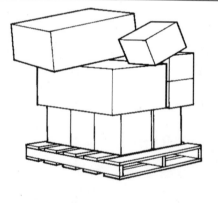

_____

_____

_____

4.

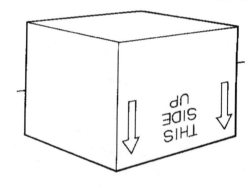

_____

_____

_____

Step 2: Discuss the questions below with a partner. Write your answers on the lines.

1. How do different racks make goods look attractive?

_____

_____

2. Retail stores are always changing their displays. Why is it important to change displays?

_____

_____

Check Your Understanding

Step 1: What do you say to be sure you understand a direction? Circle the letter of the best response.

1. The boss says, "Put three rounders in the back."
   a. Would you like me to separate them by color, vendor, or size?
   b. Do you want them on the wall?
   c. Do you want me to change the clothes on the mannequins?

2. The boss says, "We need four waterfall racks on the walls."
   a. Would you like them up there, by the shelves on the wall?
   b. Would you like me to separate them by color or by vendor?
   c. Would you like me to bring in the rolling rack?

3. The boss says, "We have to separate the merchandise on those racks."
   a. Which are the sale items?
   b. Would you like them over there?
   c. Would you like me to separate them by vendor?

4. The boss says, "Call Loss Prevention if the shipment is not right."
   a. Should I call them if only one item is missing in a case, or if a case is missing?
   b. What time is my break today?
   c. Should I put two sensors on these bottles of perfume?

5. The boss says, "Unload that truck right now."
   a. Should I unload that truck?
   b. Should I take an empty pallet onto the truck with me?
   c. Should I work late today?

Step 2: What does a good stock worker do? Put a check mark next to the words that tell what a good stock worker does.

1. _____ moves racks to set up for the big sale.

2. _____ asks questions to make sure what the boss wants done.

3. _____ puts sensors on the floor and not on merchandise.

4. _____ calls Loss Prevention when a shipment is not correct.

5. _____ puts the box cutter in the safety position when finished.

6. _____ leaves the stockroom aisle full of boxes.

7. _____ never works as a team with other workers.

8. _____ loads the hand truck as high as possible before moving.

9. _____ avoids cracks in the ground when using a pallet jack or hand truck.

10. _____ stacks larger boxes on top of smaller cases.

Complete activities 1 and 2 in class. Then do activity 3 or 4 outside of class.

1. Imagine that you are a stock worker for a large store. What do you like about your job? What do you dislike?

2. Discuss these questions with a group:
    *   Have you ever handled stock? If so, what did you like and dislike about it?
    *   Do you like to work with equipment and machinery? Why?
    *   Do you like jobs that have a lot of responsibility, such as stock jobs?
    *   Do you prefer to work with merchandise rather than customers?

3. Go to a business where there is a receiving area, or think about a time when you have seen unloading of trailers or moving of stock. Answer these questions on other paper:
    *   What kinds of equipment for unloading did you see?
    *   How did the business recycle packing material?
    *   Did the business keep the receiving area clean? Explain.
    *   How many workers did you see? What were they doing?

4. Call a local retail store to find out what qualifications a person needs to be hired in the stock department. Share with your partner what you learn.

Notes

_____

_____

_____

_____

_____

_____

_____

_____

_____

_____

_____

Unit 7
CLEANUP ON AISLE 10B

Read the words in the box. Underline the words you know. Then look at the picture. Why does the shopper look upset? What are the workers doing?

Words to Know

broom	fumes	product	(to) mix
brush	gases	safety	(to) mop (up)
caution sign	gloves	sink	(to) put up
ceiling panel	junk	voice	(to) slip
chemical	label		(to) stand back
cleanup	ladder	broken	(to) trip
common sense	maintenance worker	burned-out	(to) unplug
drain cleaner	mess	dangerous	(to) wrap
Dumpster	mop	loose	
dustpan	mop bucket		be careful
fault	piece	(to) be plugged up	I'll take care of it.
fire extinguisher	plunger	(to) fall	up-to-date
fluorescent tube		(to) get hurt	

Listen and Speak

Step 1: Listen as your teacher reads the conversation. A customer at Valueland Supermarket pushed her cart into a food display. Jack, Martha, and Tom are maintenance workers at the supermarket. Mr. Ramos is their manager.

Voice: Cleanup on aisle 10B!

Customer: [to Mr. Ramos] I'm so sorry. It was my fault. Let me help clean up the mess and pay for it.

Mr. Ramos: No, that's OK. You don't need to pay. And we don't want you to get hurt. Please stand back. There's broken glass everywhere.

Jack: I have the brush, broom, and dustpan. Martha has the mop and mop bucket.

Mr. Ramos: Be sure to wear your safety gloves. Wrap the pieces of broken glass in newspaper to throw in the Dumpster out back.

Martha: I'll put up caution signs after I mop the floor.

Mr. Ramos: Very good. We don't want anyone to slip and fall.

LATER

Mr. Ramos: [to Jack and Martha] Thanks for handling the cleanup so quickly. Now, Jack, get a ladder. There's a loose ceiling panel to fix and a burned-out fluorescent tube to replace.

Jack: I'll do it right now, Mr. Ramos. I have safety glasses for my eyes.

Mr. Ramos: Good, Jack. Martha, the sink is plugged up. Could you unplug it with the plunger? If that doesn't fix it, try drain cleaner. But read the product label and use common sense. Don't mix any chemicals or cleaning products. We don't want any dangerous fumes or gases around here.

Martha: I'll take care of it, Mr. Ramos. I'll be careful.

Mr. Ramos: OK. And please get back to me on that. I need to keep up-to-date. Thanks.

Tom: Excuse me, Mr. Ramos. I straightened up the stockroom. I moved the boxes that were blocking the fire extinguisher. Now we can get to it. And now no one will trip and fall on junk.

Mr. Ramos: Excellent. We need quick and easy access to the extinguisher in case of fire. And we don't want anyone tripping and falling. It's safety first in this store. Good work, Tom.

Step 2: Read the conversation in a small group.

Step 3: Answer these questions in your group:

- Why does Mr. Ramos tell the customer not to clean up the mess?
- What can happen if cleaning products or chemicals are mixed?

Practice

Write the correct word from the word list under each picture.

broom	Dumpster	mop	safety gloves
brush	dustpan	mop bucket	sink
caution sign	fluorescent tube	plunger	
drain cleaner	ladder	safety glasses	

1.
_____

2.
_____

3.
_____

4.
_____

5.
_____

6.
_____

7.
_____

8.
_____

9.
_____

10.
_____

11.
_____

12.
_____

13.
_____

14.
_____

Build Your Vocabulary

Words to Know

chart	paper towel	vanity	assigned
convenience	plastic liner	waste container	essential
custodial worker	restroom		proud
dispenser	soap	(to) check off	sanitary
hazard	stall	(to) empty	sparkling
initials	toilet	(to) overflow	
inspection	toilet seat cover	(to) provide	out of order
liner	toilet tissue	(to) stock	out of service
mirror	urinal		

Read what the manager of Five Streets Mall says below. She is speaking to new maintenance and custodial workers.

"We're proud to provide clean, sanitary, and attractive restrooms for our customers. You're essential to making this happen. I know you'll do a good job. When you check the restrooms at your assigned hours, you must always do the following:

- Stock the dispensers for toilet tissue, toilet seat covers, paper towels, and soap.
- Empty all of the waste containers. Replace the plastic liners when they're dirty.
- Make sure the floor is clean and dry. If it is not, put up a caution sign. A wet floor is a safety hazard.
- Check to see that the toilets and urinals are clean and are in working condition.
- Clean all mirrors, vanities, and counters. Everything should be sparkling.
- Put an out-of-order sign on the door of a restroom stall if the toilet isn't working. If a toilet overflows, mop up the water right away.
- If a restroom needs major work, put the out-of-service sign outside the entrance.

You have a copy of our Restroom Inspection Chart. This chart is also on the back of the door to each restroom. After you complete your inspection, write the time on the chart. Then check off what you did and put your initials on the chart. Remember, we do all of this for the convenience of our customers. Our customers are the reason we're here."

Pardon the inconvenience. This restroom is temporarily out of service.

Practice

Step 1:   Read the Restroom Inspection Chart below.

CLEAN RESTROOM INSPECTION

Day: _Monday_   Date: _5-17_

We are happy to provide clean and sanitary restroom facilities for our shoppers.
If this restroom is not clean or adequately stocked, please notify the management or any sales associate. Thank you.

Time	Toilet tissue Toilet seat cover dispenser stocked	Soap dispenser working/stocked	Paper towel dispensers working/stocked	Floor clean and dry	Waste container empty/clean	Toilets/Urinals working/cleaned	Vanities and Mirrors cleaned	Initials
9 A.M.	✓	✓	✓	✓	✓	✓	✓	RK
10 A.M.			X		X			MG
11 A.M.	✓			✓		✓		RK
12 P.M.	✓	✓			✓		✓	JJ
1 P.M.	X		X	X	X	X		MG
2 P.M.	✓	X	✓					RK

Step 2:   Answer the questions below. Write your answers on the lines.

1. What is the date on the Restroom Inspection Chart? _____

2. Were the paper towels stocked at 9 A.M.? _____

3. Was the toilet tissue stocked at 10 A.M.? _____

4. What was the last time the soap dispensers were filled? _____

5. What were the initials of the person who checked the restroom at 11 A.M.? _____

6. Did the worker with the initials JJ stock the toilet seat cover dispensers? _____

Listen and Speak

Words to Know

assignment	supply cabinet	(to) lift	still
clarification	vacuum	(to) red-tag	
container		(to) vacuum	elbow grease
graffiti	(to) bend		I'll get to it right
image	(to) clarify	defective	away.
lounge	(to) count on	shorthanded	on the count of . . .
muscle	(someone)	exactly	
solvent			

Step 1: Listen as your teacher reads the conversation. Jesse and Paula are custodial workers. Ms. Jones is their manager.

Jesse: Hi, Paula. Do you need any help? I finished the assignments on my to-do list, and I still have time left before my break.

Paula: Thanks for asking. I need help lifting this container. It's too heavy for one person, and I don't want to hurt my back.

Jesse: Sure. Here, I'll stand on this side. Bend at your knees and lift with your leg muscles. We'll start on the count of three—one, two, three. There, we did it.

Paula: Thanks. Can you also help me with this ladder? It's defective. Please red-tag it so no one gets hurt. I don't have time. I have to clean up the staff lounge now.

Jesse: No problem. Don't worry. I'll take care of it.

Paula: Thanks. You're a big help.

LATER

Ms. Jones: Jesse, we're shorthanded this afternoon. I need you to vacuum all of the fitting rooms. But first, change the bag in the vacuum. It's full.

Jesse: Certainly, Ms. Jones. I'll get to it right away.

Ms. Jones: Great. After you do that, could you take care of the graffiti on the men's restroom door? It gives the store a bad image.

Jesse: Could you please clarify that for me? What exactly should I do?

Ms. Jones: I'm glad you asked. I want you to remove the graffiti on the door with a cleaning solvent. It will take elbow grease. I know I can count on you to get the job done.

Jesse: Yes, you can. Paula, do you know where the vacuum bags are?

Paula: They're in the supply cabinet. It was good you asked for clarification.

Jesse: Yes. I thought she wanted me to paint the door! Paula, can you help me change the vacuum bag? I've never done that before.

Paula: I'll show you how. We're a good team. We help each other.

Step 2: Read the conversation in a group of three students.

Practice

Step 1:   Circle *T* if the sentence is true and *F* if it is false.

1. Jesse asks Paula if she needs any help.   T   F
2. Paula asks Jesse to help her clean the staff lounge.   T   F
3. To lift a heavy container, bend your knees and lift with your
   leg muscles.   T   F
4. You can hurt your back if you lift a heavy container without any help.   T   F
5. Jesse asks Paula to do him a favor.   T   F
6. Jesse says he'll red-tag the defective ladder.   T   F
7. The manager tells Jesse that they are shorthanded for the afternoon.   T   F
8. *Shorthanded* means that there are too many employees working.   T   F
9. The manager asks Jesse to change the vacuum bag after he
   vacuums the room.   T   F
10. The manager asks Jesse to paint over the graffiti on the
    men's rest room door.   T   F
11. The manager says that the graffiti gives the store a bad image.   T   F
12. Paula asks the manager to clarify exactly what she wants
    Jesse to do.   T   F
13. The manager says she knows she can count on Jesse to get
    the job done.   T   F
14. Paula tells Jesse it was good that he asked the manager
    for clarification.   T   F
15. Paula says she and Jesse are a good team.   T   F

Step 2:   What do you say? Draw a line from what you want to say on the left to the
            words you can use on the right.

1. You want to know if your co-worker
   wants help.
2. You want to thank your co-worker
   for his or her help.
3. You want your co-worker to help
   you.
4. You want the manager to explain
   again what you have to do.
5. You want the manager to know that
   you'll do what he or she wants.
6. You want your co-worker to know
   that you'll help her or him learn to
   do something new.
7. You want to tell your co-worker that
   you think the two of you work well
   together.

a. Can you do me a favor?
b. I'll get to it right away.
c. Do you need any help?
d. We're a good team.
e. Could you please clarify that for me?
f. Thanks for helping.
g. Don't worry. I'll show you how.

Be a Good Worker

Step 1: Read the information below. It is for new workers in the maintenance department at Five Streets Mall. The information is about using ladders.

"It is important to use ladders safely. These are the rules to follow for safe and proper ladder use:

- Always use a ladder instead of standing on a box, chair, or table.
- Inspect a ladder before you use it to see that it is safe.
- When using a stepladder, make sure the legs are fully extended and locked in place.
- Rest all four legs of a stepladder firmly on the floor. Make sure a ladder is steady before you step on it. Have someone hold the ladder if it is unsteady.
- Grip ladder rungs and handrails firmly. Place the heels of your shoes securely on the ladder rungs. Make sure your shoes are free from mud and grease first.
- Never stand on the top step of a ladder. Never lean too far to one side or the other.
- Never place a ladder in front of a doorway. That is a safety hazard.
- Never climb on a ladder when another person is on it.
- Never leave tools on a ladder. The tools could fall on a person moving the ladder.
- Report all injuries, no matter how small, to your supervisor. Be sure to fill out an Accident Report Form if you get hurt.
- By following safety rules, you can prevent accidents."

ACCIDENTS
Can Be Prevented

Step 2: Look at the pictures below. Write an *X* over the pictures that show people who are not using ladders safely.

1.

3.

2.

4.

Have Some Fun!

Step 1:   The scrambled words below also appear in the word box on this page. Unscramble the words and write them on the lines below.

1. pom _____

2. opsa _____

3. irmror _____

4. ssgla _____

5. addrle _____

6. muuacv _____

7. lorof _____

8. atccidne _____

access	defective	graffiti	slip
accident	dirty	ladder	soap
broken	dispenser	mirror	stock
caution	dustpan	mop	toilet
chemical	empty	restroom	trash
clean	floor	safety	vacuum
convenience	fumes	sanitary	
dangerous	glass		

Step 2:   Circle the words from the box in the puzzle below. The words may be horizontal, vertical, or diagonal. They may even be backward. Can you find them all?

```
A X A T R A S H T S E M U F Z
N C C H S P C I S E A C X L I
A O C U G O P S L V T O S O M
E P I E Q C A U T I O N A O S
L R D E S L B P H T U V F R A
C U E A G S U Q I C R E E M N
M L N E K O R B A E D N T O I
A I T I F F A R G F U I Y O T
Z U B R O M I T M E S E R R A
D A N G E R O U S D T N L T R
K L I X O P U P Y O P C U S Y
C H E M I C A L T M A E Z E S
O S T L A D I S P E N S E R T
T I S V N R V I M I R R O R P
S T O I L E T R E D D A L L A
```

Think It Over

Step 1: **Step 1:** With a partner, read the safety information below.

In matters of safety, all employees should use common sense. Using common sense means thinking before you act. It means being careful and paying attention to what you are doing at all times. It also means reporting unsafe conditions and equipment.

Step 2: Put a check mark in front of the rules that show common sense.

_____ 1. Mop up spilled liquids immediately so no one will slip and fall.

_____ 2. Never mix cleaning products or chemicals.

_____ 3. Read all product labels carefully.

_____ 4. Bend at the knees and never at the waist when you pick up a heavy object.

_____ 5. Use safety glasses when necessary.

_____ 6. Do not leave objects on the floor where someone could trip and fall.

_____ 7. Use safety gloves to pick up broken glass.

_____ 8. Make sure there is quick and easy access to all fire extinguishers.

_____ 9. Be careful using ladders.

_____ 10. Report all accidents immediately.

Step 3: How many safety hazards are in the picture below? Write them on a piece of paper. Then compare your list with your partner's list.

Make Your Mark in Retail Jobs

Check Your Understanding

Step 1:   Answer the following questions. You can find the answers in this unit.

1. The floor is wet. You do not want anyone to slip and fall. What do you say? _____
_____

2. You want to tell your supervisor that you will take care of a problem. What do you say?
_____

3. You want to know if your co-worker needs any help. What do you say? _____
_____

4. You want your co-worker to help you. What do you say? _____
_____

5. You want to thank your co-worker for helping you. What do you say? _____
_____

6. You do not understand exactly what your supervisor wants you to do. What do you say
to get clarification? _____
_____

Step 2:   You are assigned to keep the restroom clean. Draw a line from the situation
on the left to what you could do on the right. You may use some of the
sentences on the right more than once.

1. The waste containers are full.

2. The floor is wet.

3. There are no paper towels in the
dispensers.

4. There is no toilet paper in the
dispensers.

5. There is no soap in the dispensers.

6. The restroom needs major cleaning.

7. The mirrors are dirty.

8. The vanities and counters are dirty.

9. The toilets are dirty.

10. A toilet is not working.

a. I clean them.

b. I empty them.

c. I put up a caution sign.

d. I put an "out-of-order" sign on the stall
door.

e. I stock them.

f. I put up a sign saying, "This restroom is
temporarily out of service."

Complete three of the activities below. Write your answers on another sheet of paper.

1. Work with a partner. You and your partner are employees at a retail store. A co-worker calls in sick, so you will have to work shorthanded. You and your partner must do the work that three people usually do. You will have to clean the restrooms and staff lounge, vacuum the fitting rooms, and handle any emergencies. How will you and your partner work as a team to get the work done? Make a list to explain who will do what. Then share your list with the class. Explain the decisions you made.

2. Work with a partner. Discuss these questions about work safety. Then write your answers.

   • Why is safety especially important for maintenance and custodial workers?

   • What do you think are the most important safety rules for these workers to remember?

   • Which safety rules are important for home, too?

3. How important are clean restrooms to you when you are shopping? Have you ever been in a store or a mall restroom that was not clean? If so, what did you do? Did you say anything to the management?

4. Workers in the retail business must be able to handle a lot of direct supervision. Do you like to work under direct supervision? Explain your answer in writing. Include reasons or examples that support your answer.

5. Go to a public restroom in a store or a mall. Answer the questions below. Then share your report with your group.

   • Do you see an inspection chart in the restroom?

   • Is the restroom clean?

   • Does the restroom have toilet tissue, toilet seat covers, paper towels, and soap?

6. Talk to two or more maintenance or custodial workers in the retail business. Ask the following questions and write down their answers. Then share the information with your class.

   • What do the workers like best about their jobs?

   • What are the hardest parts of their jobs?

   • What is the starting salary for maintenance or custodial workers?

   • What salary can these workers earn when they have more experience?

Unit 8
MAY I HAVE YOUR ORDER?

SPECIALTY CATALOGS

Look at the picture. What type of business is shown? Why are the people waiting in line? What words from the box below help you understand the picture?

Words to Know

answer	order	(to) come to	convenient
approval	system	(to) order	immediate
associate	vitamin	(to) notice	terrific
bike shorts	workout clothes	(to) pay	
catalog		(to) spell	on sale
credit limit	(to) be in	(to) submit	You've got it.
deal	(to) call in		

Listen and Speak

Step 1: **Listen as your teacher reads the conversation. Jerry is a catalog sales associate. He is helping a customer.**

Jerry: Good morning. How may I help you?

Customer: Hi. I want to pick up my order. It was supposed to be ready today.

Jerry: What is your order number, ma'am?

Customer: I don't know. I forgot to bring it.

Jerry: That's OK. I can find it in the system under your last name. Will you spell it for me, please?

Customer: It's Nguyen. That's *N* as in *navy*, *g* as in *George*, *u-y-e-n*. My first name is Duong, or Donna. I don't remember which name I gave.

Jerry: 198 Water View Street, Surf City, right? Your telephone number please?

Customer: That's it. You've got it. And my phone number is (828) 555-1768.

Jerry: (828) 555-1768. Thanks. You ordered vitamins and workout clothes, right?

Customer: Right. You have a lot of exercise merchandise in the catalog.

Jerry: Yes, we do. Well, I'll go get your order now. I'll be right back.

A MINUTE LATER

Jerry: You ordered *one* pair of bike shorts, right? There are two pairs inside the bag.

Customer: Yes, only one pair.

Jerry: OK. [*removes one pair of shorts from bag*] We have bike shirts on sale. Notice the special here in our sale catalog.

Customer: I didn't see that. That's a great deal. I'll get one of those in medium.

Jerry: Will you put that on your D&L charge account, Ms. Nguyen?

Customer: I don't have an account here. I'll pay by check.

Jerry: I can submit an application for immediate approval if you'd like me to. It's a very convenient way to pay, and you'll get an answer in about three minutes.

Customer: Sure. I'll fill out an application.

Jerry: Great! I'll order your bike shirt while you fill out this application. Then I'll call it in.

LATER

Jerry: That comes to $37.73 including tax. You can put it on your new credit account. Your application has been approved with a credit limit of $250.00. Your new order will be here in two days. Your order number is 512B6.

Customer: Great! Thanks a lot. Where do I sign?

Jerry: Right here, by the *X*. Thank you very much, Ms. Nguyen. Have a great day.

Step 2: **Read the conversation with a partner. Then discuss your answer to this question: Is Jerry a good catalog sales associate?**

Draw a line from the question on the left to the best answer on the right.

1. How may I help you?
2. What is your order number?
3. What is on sale this month?
4. Will you spell your name, please?
5. What is your telephone number?
6. Are shoes for sale in this catalog?
7. Will you put that on your charge account?
8. How much is my order?

a. No, thank you. I'll pay cash.
b. It comes to $11.88 today.
c. It's *P* as in *Paul*, a-c-h-e-c-o.
d. I'd like to pick up my order.
e. I don't know. I forgot to write it down.
f. (828)-555-1768.
g. Yes. They're on pages 8 and 9.
h. Here's our sale catalog. Check out the good deals.

How Do You Spell That?

Step 1: Practice these short conversations with a partner.

Salesclerk: What's the last name, please?
Customer: Duvalier.
Salesclerk: Is that *D* as in *David* or *B* as in *boy*?
Customer: *D* as in *David*, u-v, as in *victory*, a-l-i-e-r.
Salesclerk: Thank you.

Salesclerk: What's your last name, please?
Customer: Mitsui.
Salesclerk: How do you spell that?
Customer: *M* as in *Mary*, i-t-s-u-i.
Salesclerk: Thank you.

Step 2: Practice this short conversation with a partner, using your own last name.

Customer: My last name is _____.
You: How do you spell that?
Customer: _____.

Unit 8: May I Have Your Order? **87**

Build Your Vocabulary

Step 1: Read about Jerry's job.

Jerry works in the Davis and Landau Catalog Store. He takes orders from customers. Usually there is a line of customers, and all are in a hurry. They do not like to wait, so Jerry works fast. He smiles when he greets customers. He gives his full attention to each one. He listens and works carefully. If he does not know an answer to a question, he asks the manager or another worker. He wants to solve the customers' problems. He is tactful and polite when he helps customers.

Jerry is a seasonal worker. He was hired to work just for the holidays. He has worked in this department for only a month, so he is still learning. When he is not busy with customers, he reviews training programs on his computer terminal.

Customers at the catalog counter usually want to pick up an order. Jerry checks his computer to see if the order is in and to find out where it is in the stockroom. Then he quickly brings the order out from the stockroom. He double-checks the order to be sure it is correct.

Sometimes Jerry can sell customers something else while he is giving them service. That is called a *point-of-service*, or POS, sale. The store gives him a commission on each POS sale he makes.

Sometimes customers want to order items in person. Then Jerry checks the availability of the items on his computer screen. He tells the customers immediately if he cannot fill the orders. Then he repeats the orders to the customers. If a customer does not have a store credit card, he invites the person to fill out an application. If the credit is approved, Jerry can receive a commission or a prize.

Jerry's customers get good service. They are satisfied and think, "I'll order again sometime." His manager is happy, too. She thinks Jerry is a "go-getter." She wants to make Jerry a permanent worker after the holiday season.

Step 2: Answer these questions about Jerry's job.

- **What does Jerry do when he is not busy with customers?**
- **Why do you think Jerry wants to make point-of-service sales?**
- **Why will Jerry's manager make him a permanent worker?**

Practice

Step 1: Put the sentences in order by placing the numbers 1 through 6 on the lines below.

1. _____ Jerry gives his full attention to each customer.
2. _____ He double-checks the order to be sure it is correct.
3. _____ The customers stand in line while they wait.
4. _____ Then Jerry quickly brings the order out from the stockroom.
5. _____ Jerry checks his computer to see if the order is in and to find out where it is in the stockroom.
6. _____ Jerry smiles when he greets customers.

Step 2: Circle the number of each sentence that is correct.

1. Jerry works fast.
2. The customers like to wait.
3. Jerry earns commission on some sales.
4. He gives part of his attention to every customer.
5. Jerry listens and works carefully.
6. He does not want to solve the customers' problems.
7. Jerry reviews training programs when he's not busy.
8. He never tries to open credit accounts for customers.
9. Jerry likes to earn a commission on each point-of-service sale.
10. He double-checks the customers' orders.
11. Jerry's customers are satisfied.
12. Jerry's manager thinks he is a "go-getter."

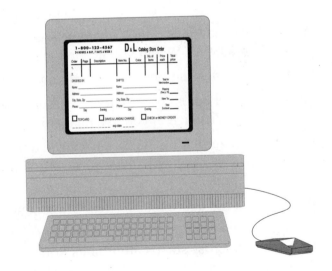

Listen and Speak

Words to Know

cross street	turtleneck	(to) deliver	available
delivery	tweed	(to) figure	heather
distance	weight	(to) go by	olive
love seat		(to) place (an order)	rust
monitor	(to) be delivered	(to) scroll (down	
sofa	(to) bring up (on a	or up)	
sweater	computer)		

Step 1: Listen as your teacher reads the conversation. Anna is taking telephone orders.

Anna: Good evening, D&L Catalog Store. May I have your first order, please?

Caller: Hello. I'd like to place an order for PL10725, size large, in red.

Anna: Let me bring that up on the monitor. That's the men's turtleneck sweater. I'm sorry, that's out of stock. We have it in red in medium or extra large.

Caller: No, it has to be large. Do you have it in another color?

Anna: I'll scroll down and check. Yes. We have it in olive, black, or rust in large.

Caller: OK. I'll take it in rust. Please check on a sofa, FF46901, in heather tweed.

Anna: That love seat is available. It can be delivered within ten days.

Caller: Love seat? No, I want the three-person sofa.

Anna: Oh, I think you want FF46900. There's a picture of it on page 289 of the catalog.

Caller: Yes, that's the one. I'd like to order that sofa, and that will be all.

Anna: OK. So that's PL10725, men's large, in rust at $29.95, and FF46900 in heather tweed at $368.95. Would you like to pick it up or shall we deliver to your home?

Caller: Are there shipping charges to my home?

Anna: There are shipping charges either to your home or to a store. It goes by weight and distance. If you live near a store, home delivery costs about the same.

Caller: Deliver it to my home. My name and address are P.R. Jazinski, *J* as in *July, a-z-i-n-s-k-i,* 3076 Well Way, Apt. 3B, Surf City. My phone number is (555) 555-1606.

Anna: Let me figure the charges. OK. It comes to $452.68, including tax and shipping. What is the nearest cross street? Also, how would you like to pay?

Caller: The cross streets are Adams Boulevard and First Street. And I'll charge it to my account, number 31B-22-4059. When will that arrive?

Anna: We'll send it out in seven to ten days. The number to call for a delivery time is 555-2122. Thank you for shopping at D&L, Ms. Jazinski. Good night.

Step 2: Read the conversation with your partner.

Step 1: Put a check mark next to what Anna does at work.

1. _____ She says, "Good evening. D&L Catalog Store."

2. _____ She takes orders from customers.

3. _____ She never says, "Please."

4. _____ She repeats the orders.

5. _____ She asks, "Shall we deliver your order or will you pick it up?"

6. _____ She never takes orders from callers.

7. _____ She asks questions about the orders.

8. _____ Anna never asks a caller for the name and address.

9. _____ She never tells the customers how much to pay.

10. _____ She says, "Thank you for shopping at D&L."

Adventurer Timepiece
HB41340
$54.99
kdjf;aairpoqiru anv adj;flakj akjdfloaisjdfpoaisudfpo lakjdpaoieu van

Data Digital Watch $49.99
HA32400
kdjf;aairpoqiru anv adj;flakjdf;oaijsdfloaiuf akjdfloaisjdfpoaisudhaksj djaoijoaigowi ;wefapoj qpowoi[qp9wi[q09w[q

Tuxedo Timepiece
$99.99 HA32400
kdjf;aairpoqiru anv adj;flakjdf;oaijsdfloaiufhjrtyjrbybrhr akjdfloaisjdfpoaisudfpoaiudf lakjdpaoieu vanbtyhty tyurtyhry

Captain's Timepiece
HC40444
$89.95
kdjf;aairpoqiru anv adj;flakjdf;oaijsdfloaiuf akjdfloaisjdfpoaisudfpoaiudf lakjdpaoieu van

Topcard 555 0006 222

Davis & Landau 555 0006 222

To place an order call
1-800-555-4567

Step 2: You are a catalog sales associate. Work with a partner to complete the conversation below. Use the catalog page shown as a guide. Then practice the completed conversation with a partner.

You: Good evening, D&L Catalog Store. May I have your first order, please?

Customer: Hello. I'd like to order the "Captain's Timepiece" in the holiday catalog.

You: _____?

Customer: It's item number HC40444, $89.95.

You: _____?

Customer: Yes. That's right.

You: _____?

Customer: I'll pick it up.

You: _____?

Customer: It's Mary Schmidt. *S* as in *Sam, c-h-m-i-d-t.* My phone number is 555-1607.

You: _____?

Customer: Thank you.

You: You're welcome. Thank you for shopping at D&L. Good-bye.

Be a Good Worker

Step 1: Jerry wants to be pleasant and helpful to all of his customers, including people on the telephone. He is learning telephone skills on his computer monitor. Read about telephone methods and manners.

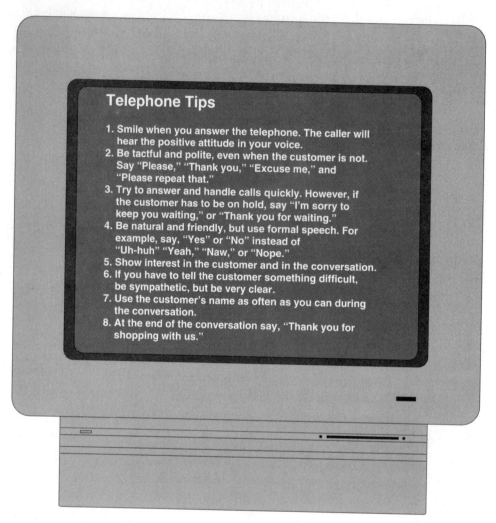

Telephone Tips

1. Smile when you answer the telephone. The caller will hear the positive attitude in your voice.
2. Be tactful and polite, even when the customer is not. Say "Please," "Thank you," "Excuse me," and "Please repeat that."
3. Try to answer and handle calls quickly. However, if the customer has to be on hold, say "I'm sorry to keep you waiting," or "Thank you for waiting."
4. Be natural and friendly, but use formal speech. For example, say, "Yes" or "No" instead of "Uh-huh" "Yeah," "Naw," or "Nope."
5. Show interest in the customer and in the conversation.
6. If you have to tell the customer something difficult, be sympathetic, but be very clear.
7. Use the customer's name as often as you can during the conversation.
8. At the end of the conversation say, "Thank you for shopping with us."

Step 2: Work with a partner. Circle the letter of the best telephone response.

1. **a.** OK. I'm ready to help you now.
   b. Thank you for waiting. May I have your order?

2. **a.** Nope. That's out of stock. Too bad.
   b. No sir, that's out of stock. I'm sorry.

3. **a.** You can't talk to me like that. Good-bye.
   b. Excuse me. Will you please repeat that? I'll try to solve the problem.

4. **a.** I'm sorry, but you can't use your charge account until next April. Would you like to pay by check?
   b. Naw. You can't charge anything here. You have bad credit.

5. **a.** OK. Good-bye.
   b. Good-bye, Ms. Gluck. Thank you for shopping at D&L Catalog Store.

Have Some Fun!

Use the words in the box to fill in the spaces in the puzzle.

application	credit	limit	promote
approved	cross street	on sale	sell
catalog	double-check	order	spell

Across

4. Your _____ comes to $17.76.
6. Would you like to fill out an _____ ?
8. Your _____ limit is $250.00.
10. What's the nearest _____ to your street?
12. We _____ hundreds of items through our catalog.

Down

1. _____ the order when you bring it out of the stockroom.
2. Your application for credit has been _____.
3. There are many half-priced items _____ in our catalog.
5. Your credit _____ is $250.00.
7. There's a picture of it on page 289 of the _____ .
9. The manager thinks the good worker is a go- _____ .
11. Will you _____ your last name, please?

Think It Over

Step 1: Work with a partner. One of you is a catalog sales associate, and the other is the customer. Write a conversation on the lines below. Make up all the information you need. The associate should suggest another item to buy or invite the customer to open a credit account.

Sales Associate: _____

Customer: _____

Sales Associate: _____

Customer: _____

Sales Associate: _____

Customer: _____

Sales Associate: _____

Customer: _____

Sales Associate: _____

Customer: _____

Sales Associate: _____

Customer: _____

Step 2: Role-play the completed conversation with your partner. Then change roles and role-play it again.

Step 3: Draw a line from what the customer says to the catalog sales associate's best response.

Customer:
1. I've been on hold for three minutes.
2. What's the matter with you? I told you already.
3. Does that come in blue?
4. Oh, I see. I have to pay by cash or check if I get it now.
5. That'll be all for today.

Catalog Sales Associate:
a. I'm sorry to keep you waiting. We're very busy. May I help you?
b. Thank you for shopping at D&L Catalog Store, sir.
c. Yes, that's right. But you can use your credit card again in three months.
d. I'm sorry. Will you please repeat the information?
e. Yes. The color is sky blue. It also comes in green, gray, or rose.

Check Your Understanding

Circle *T* if the sentence is true and *F* if it is false.

1. A catalog sales associate should relax and work slowly when a lot of customers are waiting.   T   F

2. Good workers double-check orders before giving them to customers.   T   F

3. Sales associates who are go-getters try to help customers buy merchandise and open store credit accounts.   T   F

4. Associates must never check the computer to see if an order is in.   T   F

5. Workers should always greet customers with a smile.   T   F

6. For delivery, workers should never ask for the nearest cross street.   T   F

7. It is important to be pleasant and helpful to all customers, including people on the telephone.   T   F

8. When a customer has been on hold, a worker should say, "I'm sorry for the wait."   T   F

9. A good sales associate tries to solve customers' problems.   T   F

10. A good sales associate asks the manager or another worker questions if she or he does not know the correct thing to do.   T   F

What Are The Details?

Draw a line from the question on the left to the best answer on the right.

1. What is your last name?   **a.** *B* as in *boy, a-l-a-w-i*

2. How do you spell it?   **b.** 555-6262

3. What is your address?   **c.** Verdugo Oaks Lane

4. What is your nearest cross street?   **d.** Balawi

5. What is your telephone number?   **e.** 3692B

6. What is your order number?   **f.** 161 Bluff Way, Apartment C

Complete two of the activities below. Write your answers on another sheet of paper.

1. Bring catalogs to class. Practice ordering and taking orders with a partner. Use the order forms in the catalogs or the form on this page to get the information for the order.

1-800-555-4567
24 HOURS A DAY, 7 DAYS A WEEK !

D & L Catalog Store Order

Order	Page	Description	Item No.	Color	No. of items	Price each	Total price
1.							
2.							

ORDERED BY:

Name: _____

Address: _____

City, State, Zip: _____

Phone: _____
　　　Day　　　　　Evening

SHIP TO:

Name: _____

Address: _____

City, State, Zip: _____

Phone: _____
　　　Day　　　　　Evening

Total for Merchandise _____

Shipping (See p. 78) _____

Sales Tax _____

Total Enclosed _____

☐ TOPCARD　　　☐ DAVIS & LANDAU CHARGE　　　☐ CHECK or MONEY ORDER

_ _ _ _ _ _ _ _ _ _ _ _ _ _ _ _   exp. date _ _ _ _ _ _

---

2. Go to a catalog sales center and watch the workers and customers. Then answer the following questions:
   - How long did the customers wait for help?
   - Were the sales associates or the customers in a hurry?
   - Were the sales associates polite?
   - Would you like to work in a catalog store? Why or why not?

3. Look at the Telephone Tips on page 92. Which tips do you think are most important? Why? Explain your answer in writing.

4. Call two catalog sales departments and speak to the managers. Ask the following questions and share the information with your class:
   - How much money does a new catalog sales associate earn?
   - How much does an experienced sales associate earn?
   - Do sales associates earn commission for point-of-service sales?
   - How many hours must a sales associate work to receive benefits?

Unit 9
ARE YOU ACCEPTING APPLICATIONS?

Read the words in the box. Underline any words you don't know. Look at the picture. What do you think is happening? What is the woman going to do? What are the people in the background doing?

Words to Know

applicant	interview	(to) interview	successful
appointment	interviewer	(to) look forward to	
attire	math test		congratulations
challenge	opening	confidential	Please have a seat.
clinic	position	current	passed with flying
drug test	promotion	mandatory	colors
housewares	result	private	
impression		prospective	

Listen and Speak

Step 1: Listen as your teacher reads the conversation.

Anahid: Good morning. Are you accepting applications for sales associate positions? I want to apply. I understand you're hiring for the holiday season.

Clerk: Yes, we're hiring both full- and part-time seasonal help.

Anahid: I'd like to fill out an application for full-time work.

Clerk: Certainly. [*handing Anahid an application*] Please have a seat and fill this out on both sides.

Anahid: Thank you.

Clerk: It's good you came in this morning. We're not busy on Mondays and Tuesdays, so I can give you the math test next.

LATER

Marco: Good morning, Carol.

Clerk: Hello, Marco. Congratulations on your promotion to housewares manager. I'm happy for you! I know you'll be successful.

Marco: Thanks. I'm looking forward to the challenge.

LATER

Marco: [*talking to clerk on phone*] Please set up an interview for the applicant in the business attire if she passes the math test. We need a good person immediately.

Clerk: She just passed with flying colors, so I'll send her right in. [*to Anahid*] Marco Villa, our housewares manager, will interview you now about a current opening. Please go straight through that doorway to the first office on the left.

Anahid: Oh, I'll talk to an interviewer now?

Clerk: Don't be nervous. You've already made a good first impression. When you finish your interview, I'll set up an appointment for your mandatory drug test at the clinic down the street. It's free, and the results are private and confidential. All prospective employees have to do this within twenty-four hours of interviewing.

Anahid: OK. Thank you for your help.

Clerk: My pleasure. Good luck.

Step 2: Read the conversation in a group of three students.

Step 3: Discuss these questions in your group:
- How did Anahid make a good first impression? How do you know?
- Why do you think the company requires mandatory drug testing of prospective employees?

Step 1: Draw a line from the beginning of each sentence on the left to its ending on the right.

1. Are you accepting	**a.** on your promotion.
2. We're hiring	**b.** with flying colors.
3. Please have a seat and	**c.** for your help.
4. Congratulations	**d.** applications for sales positions?
5. I'm looking forward	**e.** fill out this application on both sides.
6. She passed the test	**f.** private and confidential.
7. You made a good	**g.** full- and part-time seasonal help.
8. The results of the drug test are	**h.** with the interview.
9. Thank you	**i.** to the challenge.
10. Good luck	**j.** first impression.

Step 2: Complete the conversation below. Then practice it with a partner. You may use the conversation on page 98 to help you.

Applicant: Are you accepting applications?

Clerk: Yes. _____

Applicant: I'd _____

Clerk: Certainly. _____

Applicant: Thank you.

LATER

Clerk: The manager is ready to see you.

Applicant: Oh, I'll have an interview now?

Clerk: _____

Applicant: _____

Clerk: _____

Build Your Vocabulary

Words to Know

appearance	manner	(to) impress	positive
attendance pattern	punctuality	(to) rate	sample
attitude	résumé		
background	strength	diverse	on a scale of one
body language	weakness	honest	to ten
interviewee	willingness		

Step 1: Listen as your teacher reads about Anahid's interview.

When Anahid applied for a job at Davis and Landau, she dressed in business attire because the sales associates in the store wear business clothes. She did not take friends with her; she went alone. When she filled out the application, she used the sample application form and résumé that she had brought with her. She was polite to everyone and was professional. The managers noticed Anahid because of her appearance and her actions. She made a good first impression.

When Marco interviewed Anahid, he wanted to find out if she would be a good worker. He asked the following questions:
- How would you rate your punctuality and attendance pattern on a scale of one to ten?
- How would you rate your ability to get along with people from diverse backgrounds?

He asked more questions about Anahid's experience and her availability to work. He wanted to find out about her strengths and her weaknesses. Anahid gave good answers to these questions. She told Marco about her excellent attendance record at her last job. She told him she enjoyed working with all types of people. She was honest. She looked at Marco when she spoke and used good body language. Marco liked Anahid's positive attitude, enthusiasm, and willingness to learn. She was a good interviewee, so Marco recommended that she be hired if she passed the drug test.

Marco tells all interviewees, "You don't get a second chance to make a first impression. So make sure the first impression you make is a good one." Anahid impressed Marco.

Step 2: Read the story in a group of two or three students.

Step 3: Discuss these questions in your group:
- What did Anahid say and do that impressed Marco?
- How would you answer the questions that Marco asked Anahid?
- What does "You don't get a second chance to make a first impression" mean to you?

Practice

Step 1: Put a check mark next to each sentence that tells what you can do to make a good first impression in an interview.

_____ 1. Wear sandals and a T-shirt.

_____ 2. Wear business attire.

_____ 3. Be polite to everyone you meet.

_____ 4. Go alone to apply for the job.

_____ 5. Bring lots of friends with you when you apply.

_____ 6. Fill out the application neatly and clearly.

_____ 7. Look and act professional.

_____ 8. Show enthusiasm and a positive attitude.

_____ 9. Say you do not want to take a test.

_____ 10. Don't look at people when you speak to them.

_____ 11. Make eye contact and use body language when you speak to people.

_____ 12. Show a willingness to learn.

_____ 13. Say you have experience even if you do not.

_____ 14. Answer all the questions on the application.

Step 2: The applicants below were not hired for different reasons. Read about these people. Then write *appearance, punctuality, attendance,* or *experience* to show why you think the applicant was not hired.

1.

This applicant dresses in business attire and is professional. However, she was often sick and absent from work on her previous job. She was not hired because of her _____.

2.

This applicant wants a job very badly. He is a hard worker, and he likes to help people. However, he has blue hair and colorful tattoos on his arms. He was not hired because of his

_____.

3.

This applicant has a lot of experience in retail sales. She was fired from her last job for being late several times a week. She was not hired because of her _____.

4.

This applicant is wearing business clothes and is applying for a job as a sales associate. He does not have sales experience, and he does not have a résumé. He was not hired because of his _____.

Listen and Speak

Words to Know

advancement	(to) badge in	(to) relax	go the extra mile
advice	(to) badge out	(to) succeed	keep an eye on . . .
age	(to) be on time		take pride in . . .
college	(to) bet	merchandising	
opportunity	(to) depend on	own	
review	(someone)	temporary	
reward	(to) own		

Step 1: Listen as your teacher reads the conversation.

Anahid: Hi. I'm Anahid. I'm new here. How long have you been here?

Jerry: I'm Jerry. Nice to meet you. I just had my thirty-day review. Are you seasonal help, too?

Anahid: Yes, but I hope I can stay on after the holidays.

Jerry: Me, too. It depends on us, in part. We have to do a good job and go the extra mile.

Anahid: I think if we're working, we should do our best and take pride in our work.

Jerry: I think so, too. The manager of the shoe department started just two years ago as a temporary worker. He's about our age. I bet he'll be a store manager someday.

Anahid: I'd like to have a career in retail. There's a lot of opportunity for advancement.

Jerry: I want to own my own store one day, so I want to learn all I can.

Anahid: I'm taking merchandising classes in college. There's a lot to learn about retail.

Jerry: It's hard work, but it has rewards. I find satisfaction in doing a job well.

Anahid: If you enjoy doing something, it's easier. I just finished watching the orientation videos. Now I'm training on the computers. It's fun so far.

Jerry: Yes, it is. Oh, it looks like my break is almost over. I have to go badge in.

Anahid: I have to remind myself to badge in and badge out when I take breaks or eat lunch.

Jerry: Don't worry. You'll get used to it. The important thing is to be on time.

Anahid: I'll keep my eye on my watch.

Jerry: They always say to arrive early if you want to succeed. If we're late, the store is open, the customers are here, and someone has to do our job for us. I get here a half an hour before I start work, so I can relax and get something to eat.

Anahid: That's good advice. It's been nice talking to you. Let's hope they keep us both on after the season.

Step 2: Read the conversation with a partner. Then answer these questions:
  • Why is it important to arrive early for work?
  • Do you find satisfaction when you do a job well? Explain.

Step 1: Write *T* if the sentence is true and *F* if it is false.

_____ 1. Anahid is a seasonal worker.

_____ 2. Jerry just had his thirty-day review.

_____ 3. Anahid does not want to work after the holidays.

_____ 4. Anahid wants to have a career in the retail business.

_____ 5. Jerry is taking merchandising classes in college.

_____ 6. Anahid has been watching orientation videos and is training on the computer.

_____ 7. Jerry and Anahid have to badge in and badge out for breaks.

_____ 8. Jerry says, "They always say to arrive on time if you want to succeed."

_____ 9. Sometimes Jerry is late for work.

_____ 10. Anahid thinks Jerry's advice is good.

Step 2: Look at Anahid's schedule for Saturday. Then read the sentences below. Write *badges in* or *badges out* to complete each sentence.

1. When Anahid arrives at 8:00 A.M., she _____.

2. Anahid _____ at 10:00 A.M. for her morning break.

3. At 10:15 A.M., she _____ after break.

4. Anahid _____ at 12:15 P.M. for lunch.

5. She _____ after lunch at 12:45 P.M.

6. At 2:30 P.M., she _____ for her afternoon break.

7. She _____ at 2:45 P.M. to return to work.

8. Before she goes home at 4:30 P.M., Anahid _____ .

Anahid's Saturday Schedule

8:00 A.M.	Start work
10:00 A.M. – 10:15 A.M.	Break
12:15 P.M. – 12:45 P.M.	Lunch
2:30 P.M. – 2:45 P.M.	Break
4:30 P.M.	Finish work

Be a Good Worker

Step 1: Read about how workers get noticed.

Workers who are go-getters "go the extra mile" and do more than is expected of them. They are willing to learn new skills and add responsibilities. They offer to help customers, co-workers, and supervisors.

Step 2: Are you a go-getter? Read the sentences below. Are they true for you? For each sentence, put a check mark in the *Always, Sometimes,* or *Never* column.

	Always	Sometimes	Never
1. I am on time or early for work.			
2. I have a good attendance record.			
3. I communicate clearly and politely with others.			
4. I dress in appropriate clothing for my job.			
5. I am cooperative and work as part of a team.			
6. I am reliable.			
7. I am honest and loyal.			
8. I encourage my co-workers.			
9. I like to help others solve problems.			
10. I have a positive attitude about my work.			
11. I like to learn new skills.			
12. I take pride in my work.			
13. I keep busy and do a full day's work.			
14. I help and do things for other people.			
15. I can handle responsibility.			

Step 3: Count the check marks in the columns. Give yourself two points for every *Always* answer, one point for every *Sometimes* answer, and zero points for every *Never* answer.

My Total Score

_____

How Do You Rate?

If you scored 20 to 30 points, you are a go-getter. If you scored below 20 points, try the exercise again another day.

Have Some Fun!

Circle the words from the box in the puzzle below. The words may be horizontal, vertical, or diagonal. They even may be backward.

advice	college	interview	professional
application	confidential	math	promotion
apply	congratulations	opportunity	punctuality
attendance	diverse	positive	rate
attire	hire	pride	satisfaction
background	impression	private	succeed
career			

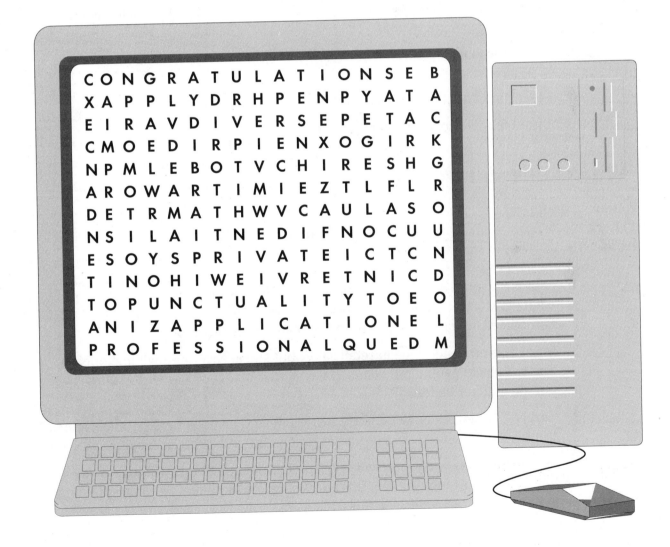

C O N G R A T U L A T I O N S E B
X A P P L Y D R H P E N P Y A T A
E I R A V D I V E R S E P E T A C
C M O E D I R P I E N X O G I R K
N P M L E B O T V C H I R E S H G
A R O W A R T I M I E Z T L F L R
D E T R M A T H W V C A U L A S O
N S I L A I T N E D I F N O C U U
E S O Y S P R I V A T E I C T C N
T I N O H I W E I V R E T N I C D
T O P U N C T U A L I T Y T O E O
A N I Z A P P L I C A T I O N E L
P R O F E S S I O N A L Q U E D M

Think It Over

Work with a small group. Discuss the ten reasons why workers give good service to their customers. Write *Yes* if you think the reason is good and *No* if you think it is not a good reason.

_____ 1. I like people, and I like to help them.

_____ 2. I have to earn money. If I do not give good service, they may fire me.

_____ 3. Giving the best service I can is a challenge. It makes my job interesting.

_____ 4. It is better than staying home and watching TV.

_____ 5. If I give good customer service, I may get a promotion or a permanent job with better benefits.

_____ 6. I like to keep busy. A busy day helping customers is better than a slow day.

_____ 7. I am learning to give good customer service because it will help me in any service job.

_____ 8. I want customers to shop here again and again, so I can make a lot of commissions.

_____ 9. I feel good about myself when I do my best.

_____ 10. I want to meet someone to marry me.

Who Will You Hire?

You are a manager, and you need a good worker for your department. Put a check mark next to the applicant you would hire below. Then tell your group why you would hire that person.

_____ 1. Sam has a lot of experience in retail sales. He has a full-time job, but he also wants to work part-time on evenings and weekends for extra money. Sometimes he has to be absent to take care of his sick mother.

_____ 2. Marie has no experience in retail sales, but she is eager and willing to learn. She is a single parent and wants to get started in a good career to support herself and her children.

_____ 3. Carl is a hard-working person. He is friendly and loves to help people. He has trouble getting hired because he has green hair and a ring in his nose.

_____ 4. Sue needs a job badly. She will take any job offered. She is willing to work hard. At her last job, she was fired for being late too often. She takes the bus to work, and sometimes she misses it.

Check Your Understanding

Complete each sentence below. Circle the letter of the correct ending.

1. When applying for a sales associate job,
   a. take your sister or brother with you.
   b. go alone.

2. When going to fill out a job application,
   a. wear business attire.
   b. wear whatever you want.

3. Seasonal workers
   a. are hired for the holidays.
   b. never work after the holiday season.

4. An interviewer asks about punctuality and attendance
   a. to find out if the person is honest.
   b. because he or she does not want a worker to be late or absent.

5. Someone who fills out an application for employment is called
   a. an employee.
   b. an applicant.

6. In the retail business, there are many opportunities
   a. to make a good first impression.
   b. for advancement.

7. A sales associate should
   a. know how to get along with people from diverse backgrounds.
   b. not try to get along with others.

8. During an interview, an interviewee should
   a. say what the interviewer wants to hear.
   b. look and act professional.

9. To be successful in the retail business,
   a. a worker should arrive early.
   b. a worker can arrive late.

10. Before taking a break, an employee should
    a. badge in.
    b. badge out.

11. A person who "goes the extra mile" to help out
    a. will make customers unhappy.
    b. will succeed in customer service.

12. A go-getter is a worker who
    a. has a positive attitude about the job.
    b. has a negative attitude about the job.

13. Good workers
    a. have had previous experience in the retail business.
    b. are willing and eager to learn new skills.

14. Some retail businesses make all prospective employees
    a. take college classes in merchandising.
    b. take a mandatory drug test.

15. Seasonal workers who want to work after the holidays
    a. should try to do more than is expected of them.
    b. should not offer to help customers, co-workers, and supervisors.

16. Someone who wants to make a good first impression shows off his or her
    a. appearance and behavior.
    b. previous experience.

Complete activities 1 and 2 with a partner. Then do activity 3 or 4 on your own.

1. If you were an interviewer, what questions would you ask an applicant? What answers would you be looking for in a good applicant? Write your questions on another sheet of paper. Then discuss your questions and answers with your partner.

2. Practice role-playing interviews with a partner. Take turns being the interviewer and interviewee. You can use the questions you wrote in activity 1. You also may want to record the interviews on audio- or videotape.

3. Visit two or three retail stores near your home to get sample employment application forms. Compare the applications. Do they ask similar questions? Share the applications with a group of three or four students. Then fill out the applications for practice.

4. Go to several retail stores to look at the type of clothes the employees are wearing. Answer the following questions:
    • Which stores have employees who wear casual clothes?
    • Which stores have employees in business attire?
    • Why do you think these stores have different dress codes for their workers?

Notes

_____
_____
_____
_____
_____
_____
_____
_____
_____
_____
_____
_____
_____
_____

Unit 10
A NEW MANAGER

Look at the picture. Who are the people? What are they doing? What do you think they are saying?

Words to Know

benefits	initiative	support	(to) work (one's way) up
brochure	leadership	tax-deferred savings plan	in-depth
clientele	management		on-the-job
customer profile	market research	(to) be eligible for	top-notch
enthusiasm	profit sharing plan	(to) maximize	
executive	staff development	(to) prepare	the sky's the limit
future	stock purchase plan		

Listen and Speak

Listen as your teacher reads the conversation between Marco Villa and Alice Kerrida, the general manager of Davis and Landau.

Alice: Congratulations on being promoted to manager, Marco.

Marco: Thank you. I'm looking forward to my new responsibilities.

Alice: You bring on-the-job experience and a strong background in customer service to your new position. You've shown initiative, enthusiasm, and leadership skills. You deserve your promotion. It's good that we promote from within.

Marco: Thank you. I appreciate the opportunity to work my way up in the company. I look forward to being on the management team.

Alice: Great. Will you start the Executive Training Program next week?

Marco: Yes. I want to learn how to maximize sales to make a profit for my department. I also want to learn about staff development and team building.

Alice: Good. One of your duties will be to give the associates in your department in-depth training to improve their sales techniques. You'll also learn how to supervise staff closely and create to-do lists for each associate.

Marco: Thank you for your support. Can you tell me about my new benefits?

Alice: Certainly. You're already part of our company health plan. Now you'll also be eligible for our stock purchase plan, our profit sharing plan, and our tax-deferred savings plan. I'll get you some brochures.

Marco: Excellent. I'd like that. Thank you.

Alice: I'd like you to do some market research. Please prepare a customer profile for your department. That way you'll know what merchandise will sell. One of our biggest challenges in the retail business is to build a strong return clientele.

Marco: I'd like to make an appointment to discuss that with you further.

Alice: Of course. Marco, I know you'll be a top-notch executive and continue to work your way up in the company. Good luck! The sky's the limit for your future!

Step 2:   Work with a partner. Read the conversation and then answer the following questions:

What does "promote from within" mean?

What new benefits will Marco have in management?

What does "build a return clientele" mean?

Why does Alice say to Marco, "The sky's the limit for your future"?

Practice

Step 1: Write *T* if the sentence is true and *F* if it is false.

_____ 1. Marco tells Alice that he is looking forward to his new benefits.

_____ 2. Alice says Marco has had a strong background in management.

_____ 3. Alice wants Marco to have initiative and enthusiasm, and she wants him to learn leadership skills.

_____ 4. Davis and Landau promotes from within.

_____ 5. Marco has been working his way up in the company.

_____ 6. Marco will be starting the Executive Training Program.

_____ 7. Marco wants to learn how to maximize sales.

_____ 8. Alice says she wants Marco to make a profit for his department.

_____ 9. Alice tells Marco one of his duties is to train associates in sales techniques.

_____ 10. The managers at Davis and Landau are eligible for a profit sharing plan.

_____ 11. Marco was not eligible to be part of a company health plan before.

_____ 12. Alice wants Marco to prepare a customer profile for his department so he will know what merchandise will sell.

_____ 13. Alice says that one of the biggest challenges in the retail business is building a team of good workers.

_____ 14. Alice thinks Marco will be a top-notch executive.

_____ 15. Alice says that the sky is the limit for Marco's future.

Step 2: Draw a line from the beginning of the sentence on the left to its ending on the right.

1. Can you tell me about
2. The sky's the limit for
3. The company promotes
4. I'm looking forward to
5. I'll get you a
6. I appreciate the opportunity
7. Thank you for

a. from within.
b. my new responsibilities.
c. your future.
d. your support.
e. brochure about your benefits.
f. my benefits?
g. to work my way up.

Build Your Vocabulary

Words to Know

emergency	scheduling	(to) request	corrective
lateness	shift	(to) run smoothly	final
notice	unit	(to) schedule	valid
problem			
schedule		absent	visually appealing

Read what Sonia and Marco are learning in management training. Sonia is the manager of the toy department, and Marco is the manager of housewares.

"Oh, John wants next weekend off. I don't know if that will be possible."

The manager schedules associates' shifts.

"Let's display the new action-toy unit in front."

The manager makes sure the merchandise is visually appealing.

A department cannot run smoothly without a work schedule that staff members follow. That is why workers need to have a valid reason if they miss work. A valid reason is a real emergency. For example, if an employee is sick, that is a valid reason to miss work. If an employee is just too tired to come to work, that is not a valid reason to be absent.

Sonia and Marco tell the associates to give two weeks' notice for special scheduling needs. If an employee needs a special day off, he or she should request it as soon as possible. If someone else has also asked for the same day off, the first person who requested it will get it. Of course, the managers have final approval for all shift changes.

"Now, Marie, your repeated lateness is a problem. How can I help you improve?"

The manager gives corrective reviews to employees who are having problems at work.

Practice

Step 1: Read what the manager says on the left. Then draw a line from what the manager says to the management skill being used on the right.

1. "You are absent too often. How can I help you to improve?"

2. "Please put the new sweaters on the rack by the register."

3. "If you need a special day off, please write down your request."

4. "The department must look attractive so the customers will shop here."

5. "I'm sorry, but you didn't give me enough notice to take tomorrow off. We need you here."

a. scheduling associates

b. displaying merchandise

c. doing employee reviews

Step 2: Read the sentences. Put a check mark in front of each sentence that shows a valid reason to miss work.

_____ 1. You hurt your back. Your doctor tells you to rest.

_____ 2. You have to go to the grocery store.

_____ 3. Your son is graduating from high school next month.

_____ 4. You have to clean your house.

_____ 5. Your baby is sick.

_____ 6. You are too tired to go to work.

_____ 7. Your car will not start.

_____ 8. You want to take the test to get your driver's license.

_____ 9. Your child had an accident at school. You have to go pick her up.

_____ 10. You want to go to the movies.

Step 3: Read each sentence below with a partner. Does the worker give enough notice for time off? For each item, write *enough notice* or *not enough notice*.

1. Richard wants to go to his brother's wedding in three weeks. _____

2. Lisa makes a dental appointment for this afternoon and asks for today off. _____

_____

3. George wants to take his son to a baseball game. He asks for a day off six weeks in advance. _____

4. Carla has final exams two months from now. She will need a week off. _____

_____

5. Jack wants to take his mother to her doctor's appointment tomorrow. _____

_____

Listen and Speak

Words to Know

absenteeism co-worker cure (to) advance (to) break up	(to) cover for (someone) (to) cut back (to) help (to) let (someone) go	(to) move up (to) pull (one's) weight bright embarrassing	fair upset I understand how you feel.

Step 1: Listen as your teacher reads the conversation.

Sonia: Gil, this is your second corrective review in a month. You're a good worker, but you were absent again. I hoped you would remain with us and even advance in the company. Now I worry that I'll have to let you go for absenteeism.

Gil: I know. I try to be here, but I'm having some personal problems.

Sonia: Are you working too many hours? I want to help. I don't want to lose you.

Gil: It's embarrassing, but I'd better tell you. My girlfriend broke up with me, and I'm very upset. I can't sleep at night, and then I'm too tired to work. I'm sorry.

Sonia: I understand how you feel, and I'm sorry. I've had the same experience myself. If you want to work here, you must leave personal problems at home. I need you here for the customers. How about cutting back your working hours?

Gil: I can't cut back. In fact, I need more hours. I have to work, and I like this job.

Sonia: Gil, being absent isn't fair to others. We have to cover for you. Everyone on our team has to work harder when we can't depend on one person. You're not pulling your weight right now. Please think about your co-workers, too.

Gil: I'm really sorry. What you're saying is right. I'm sure I can leave my problems at home. Hard work may be a cure for me. Losing my job would make my problems much worse. I want to keep my job and move up if I can.

Sonia: Gil, I'm glad you want to stay and work hard. You can have a bright future.

Step 2: Read the conversation with a partner. Then talk about it. Do you think Sonia corrected the problem? Explain.

Step 3: Another part of Sonia's job is to promote excellent workers. A good worker can become a team leader, or lead. The team leader is a role model. Other workers shadow the team leader, or follow the leader to learn a job. What do you think is more difficult, correcting employees who have problems or finding excellent employees to promote? Why?

Practice

absent bright	corrective depend	fair go	home hours	let personal	team work

Step 1: Choose from the words above to fill in the blanks.

1. Sonia tells Gil that this is his second _____ review in a month.

   He was _____ again.

2. Sonia worries that she will have to _____ Gil _____ for absenteeism.

3. Gil is having some _____ problems. Sonia offers to help

   by cutting Gil's _____.

4. Being absent is not _____ to others. Everyone on the

   _____ has to work harder when workers cannot

   _____ on one person.

5. Gil decides to leave his problems at _____.

   He thinks hard _____ may be a cure for his problem.

6. Sonia encourages Gil by saying, "You can have a _____

   future here."

Step 2: Answer the questions below. Write your answers on the lines.

1. Sonia says that Gil's a good worker, and she does not want to let him go. In what ways do you suppose he is a good worker and in what ways is he not?

   _____

   _____

   _____

2. Corrective reviews with employees are a difficult part of a manager's job. How does Sonia talk to Gil in the corrective review? Do Gil and Sonia correct the problem? Explain.

   _____

   _____

   _____

Be a Good Worker

When managers promote from within, they have to pick the best associates. Read the following statements about promoting associates.

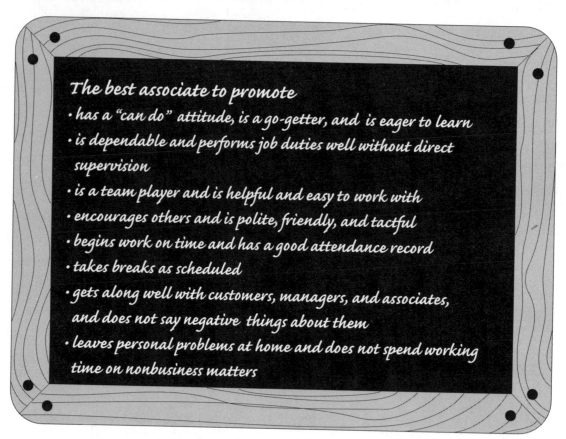

The best associate to promote
- has a "can do" attitude, is a go-getter, and is eager to learn
- is dependable and performs job duties well without direct supervision
- is a team player and is helpful and easy to work with
- encourages others and is polite, friendly, and tactful
- begins work on time and has a good attendance record
- takes breaks as scheduled
- gets along well with customers, managers, and associates, and does not say negative things about them
- leaves personal problems at home and does not spend working time on nonbusiness matters

You Are the Manager

Step 1:   You are a manager, and you need a manager trainee. Which three statements above best describe the person you want?

Step 2:   Explain why you chose the three statements you did to describe the manager trainee you want. Write your answer on the lines below.

_____

_____

_____

_____

_____

Have Some Fun!

benefits	maximize	profit	schedule
leadership	notice	promote	shadow
limit	polite	role model	valid

Use the words from the box to complete the sentences below. Then place the answers in the puzzle.

Across

2. When managers _____ from within, they pick the best associates.

4. A manager is eligible for many employee _____.

8. A way to learn a new job is to _____ a team leader or other employee.

9. "The sky's the _____" means there are unlimited opportunities for advancement.

10. The best associate is _____, friendly, and tactful.

11. An employee should have a _____ reason to be absent.

Down

1. Alice tells Marco he has shown _____ skills.

2. When a company makes money, it makes a _____.

3. To _____ sales is to increase them.

5. Managers _____ workers' time.

6. An employee must give enough _____ for special scheduling needs.

7. A _____ is an example to other workers.

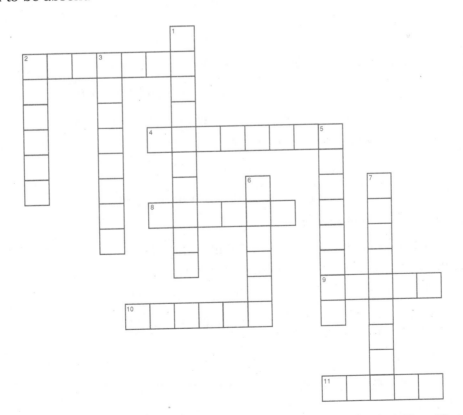

Step 1: Read about what makes a successful manager.

A successful manager must have good communication skills. The manager should be understanding and polite to employees. Sonia knows how to talk to workers. When she reviews or interviews someone, she is polite. She uses the person's name and tries to help the worker succeed. She shows that she understands.

When Sonia makes a simple request, she uses the words *could* or *would*.

Step 2: You are the manager. Read the sentences below. Put a check mark next to the statement that is the better way to communicate.

1. You want an employee to attend work regularly.

   a. _____ "I'm sick and tired of your absenteeism!"

   b. _____ "Are you working too many hours? I need you here for the customers."

2. You want to show an employee that you understand her problem.

   a. _____ "I know how you feel, and I feel bad for you."

   b. _____ "Hard work can cure your problem."

3. You want to encourage an employee to work for a promotion.

   a. _____ "The job is demanding."

   b. _____ "For team players like you, with ability and desire, there are opportunities for good money, benefits, and advancement."

4. You want a worker to help you with a merchandise display.

   a. _____ "Would you bring out the new units and display them here by the register?"

   b. _____ "Do the display now!"

Step 3: Role-play a corrective review with a partner.

Check Your Understanding

You are the manager. Respond to the situations below. Write your responses on the lines.

1. You want to congratulate an associate on her promotion. What can you say?
   _____

2. You want to tell an employee that he did not give you enough notice to take a day off. What can you say? _____
   _____

3. You want to let a worker know that you understand how he feels. What can you say? _
   _____

4. You want to tell a worker that he must have a valid reason to be off. What can you say?
   _____

5. You want to tell a worker who is often absent that she is not pulling her weight. What can you say? _____
   _____

6. You want to tell an employee that he must arrive at work on time. What can you say?
   _____

7. You want to show appreciation for the work an employee has done. What can you say?
   _____

8. You want to show an associate that you are listening carefully. What can you say or do?
   _____

9. You want to tell a worker who is having problems at work that you want to help her improve. What can you say? _____
   _____

Complete activities 1 and 2. Then choose three more activities to do. Write your answers on another sheet of paper.

1. Talk to a partner about what makes a good manager. Then make a report to your group. Answer the following questions:
   - What strengths should a good manager have?
   - How does a good manager encourage team building among associates?

2. Work in a small group. Write a list of questions to ask a salesperson about retail work and building a return clientele. Then go to a retail store and interview different salespeople. Each person should visit a different group. Next, meet with your group and talk about the answers you found. Which answers were the same? Which were different?

3. Talk to a partner about careers in the retail industry. Which careers interest you? On another sheet of paper, write a few sentences about each job to explain why you are interested in the job.

4. What are the qualities of a good retail worker? Make a list.

5. What does "working your way up" mean? Explain your answer in writing. Include examples from retail industry jobs.

6. Research one or more retail merchandising college programs in your area. Answer the following questions:
   - What courses of study does the program offer?
   - Does the program help graduates get jobs? What kinds of jobs can graduates get?
   - What is the cost to attend these programs?

Notes

_____
_____
_____
_____
_____
_____
_____
_____
_____

Words to Know

A

a lot, 18
A-frame rack, 61
absent, 112
absenteeism, 114
accessory, 16
account, 25
accurate, 52
(to) acknowledge, 40
action, 40
activity, 4
ad, 4
(to) advance, 114
advancement, 102
(to) advertise, 6
advice, 102
after all, 30
age, 102
(to) agree, 54
aisle, 1
alarm, 49
alert, 28
aloud, 28
already, 30
amount tendered, 28
angry, 40
answer, 85
anything in particular, 18
(to) apologize, 40
(to) appeal, 4
appeal, 4
appearance, 100
appliance, 16
applicant, 97
application, 25
(to) apply, 18
appointment, 97
(to) appreciate, 49
(to) apprehend, 49
(to) approach, 54
approval, 85
arm (of a rack), 61
article, 25
as a matter of fact, 49
assigned, 76
assignment, 78
assistant manager, 49
associate, 85
attendance pattern, 100
attention, 28
attire, 97
attitude, 100
attractive, 4
automatic, 6
availability, 88
available, 90
(to) avoid, 66

aware, 54

B

back, 13
back-up work, 18
background, 100
(to) badge in, 102
(to) badge out, 102
(to) balance, 30
bank, 49
bar code, 1
base, 54
(to) be authorized, 42
be careful, 73
(to) be delivered, 90
(to) be eligible for, 109
(to) be in, 85
(to) be in charge, 49
(to) be on time, 102
(to) be plugged up, 73
(to) be ready, 61
(to) belong, 4
(to) bend, 78
benefits, 109
(to) bet, 102
between, 6
bike shorts, 85
bill, 28
bin, 66
blazer, 25
body language, 100
boss, 66
both, 6
box cutter, 64
bracelet, 54
break, 16
(to) break up, 114
bright, 114
(to) bring, 61
brochure, 109
broken, 73
broom, 73
(to) browse, 18
brush, 73
built-in, 6
bunch, 66
burned-out, 73
business, 18
busy, 18
button, 6
(to) buy, 1
buy, 6
by the way, 18

C

(to) call, 18
(to) call in, 85

calm, 42
calmly, 40
camera, 6
candy, 1
cardboard, 66
(to) care, 42
(to) carry, 6
cart, 4
carton, 64
case, 6
cash, 13
cash drawer, 28
cash register, 1
cashier, 25
catalog, 85
(to) catch, 49
(to) cause, 25
caution sign, 73
ceiling panel, 73
cement, 66
chain, 4
challenge, 97
change, 1
(to) change one's mind, 25
(to) charge, 1
chart, 76
(to) check, 1
check, 25
(to) check off, 76
checking account, 25
chemical, 73
choice, 25
clarification, 78
(to) clarify, 78
(to) clean, 1
cleanup, 73
(to) clear, 42
clearance, 61
clientele, 109
clinic, 97
close, 18
(to) close (out), 49
closing time, 49
clothes, 13
co-worker, 114
coat, 42
code, 49
coin, 28
college, 102
come again, 49
(to) come first, 37
(to) come in (a style or color), 13
(to) come to, 85
(to) come with, 6
commission, 31
common sense, 73
compactor, 66

(to) complain, 40
complaint, 40
computer printout, 61
confidential, 97
congratulations, 97
container, 78
contents, 64
(to) control, 52
convenience, 76
convenient, 85
(to) convince, 37
cooperation, 49
copy, 37
correct, 28
corrective, 112
cosmetic, 1
(to) cost, 6
costume jewelry, 16
count, 52
(to) count on (someone), 78
counter, 1
counterfeit detection pen, 28
coupon, 4
(to) cover, 16
(to) cover for (someone), 114
crack, 66
(to) credit, 37
credit department, 28
credit limit, 85
cross street, 90
crystal, 66
cure, 114
curling iron, 16
currency, 30
current, 97
custodial worker, 76
customer, 1
customer profile, 109
(to) cut back, 114

D

dangerous, 73
deal, 85
(to) deal with, 40
(to) decide, 13
defective, 78
delivery, 90
denomination, 30
(to) depend on (someone), 102
deposit, 49
(to) dial, 52
difference, 6
difficult, 40
dime, 28
direction, 28

love seat, 90
lovely, 54
low, 1
lunch, 16

M

ma'am, 1
mad, 40
mail, 42
mailing list, 42
maintenance worker, 73
major, 25
make a big splash, 61
(to) make change, 28
(to) make sure, 64
mall, 49
management, 109
manager, 4
mandatory, 97
mannequin, 61
manner, 100
markdown, 52
marked down, 37
market research, 109
markup, 52
(to) match, 28
math test, 97
(to) maximize, 109
medium, 13
(to) meet, 13
meeting, 4
men's department, 13
merchandise, 16
merchandising, 102
mess, 73
metal, 66
mirror, 76
miss, 1
mistake, 37
(to) mix, 73
monitor, 90
mop, 73
(to) mop (up), 73
mop bucket, 73
(to) move, 61
(to) move up, 114
muscle, 78

N

nail polish, 1
navy, 37
neat, 4
nervous, 37
news, 4
next, 1
next to, 61
nickel, 28
no problem, 1
(to) notice, 85
notice, 112
number one, 4

O

object, 16
observant, 54
often, 4
olive, 90
on a scale of one to ten, 100
on sale, 85
on the count of . . . , 78
on the left, 61
on the right, 61
on-the-job, 109
(to) open, 4
opening, 97
operative, 52
opportunity, 102
(to) order, 85
order, 85
orientation, 28
ourselves, 4
out of order, 76
out of place, 4
out of service, 76
over there, 37
(to) overflow, 76
(to) own, 102
own, 102

P

package, 49
(to) page, 52
pallet, 66
pallet jack, 66
paper, 66
paper towel, 76
paperwork, 52
parents, 54
parking lot, 49
passed with flying
    colors, 97
patience, 49
patron, 16
(to) pay, 85
penny, 28
percent, 25
perfectly, 37
permanent, 52
personal, 52
photograph (photo), 6
(to) pick (someone) up, 54
(to) pick up, 4
piece, 73
(to) place (an order), 90
placement, 61
plaid, 25
plastic, 66
plastic liner, 76
pleasant, 40
Please have a seat., 97
plunger, 73
pocket, 6
point and shoot, 6

point-of-service sale, 88
policy, 40
polite, 40
popular, 18
position, 97
positive, 100
(to) postdate, 28
preoccupied, 54
(to) prepare, 109
price, 1
price tag, 61
private, 97
prize, 88
problem, 112
(to) proceed, 54
(to) process, 64
product, 1
profit, 52
profit sharing plan, 109
program, 88
promotion, 97
promotion (promo), 6
proper, 28
(to) prosecute, 49
prospective, 97
protection, 28
proud, 76
(to) provide, 76
pull your weight, 114
punctuality, 100
purchase, 1
(to) push, 6
(to) put (something) back, 1
(to) put aside, 18
(to) put up, 73

Q

quarter, 28
quick change artist, 30
quickly, 1

R

rack, 13
rainy, 1
(to) rate, 100
ready, 16
reason, 40
receipt, 13
receiving area, 64
recorded, 54
(to) recycle, 66
(to) red-tag, 78
refund, 42
register plate, 28
(to) relax, 102
(to) remember, 4
(to) remove, 25
(to) repeat, 40
(to) replace, 30
(to) request, 112
responsibility, 52

restroom, 76
result, 97
résumé, 100
retail industry, 52
(to) return, 37
return, 37
(to) review, 88
review, 102
reward, 102
rewind, 6
right back, 13
(to) ring up, 25
robbery, 54
roll of film, 6
rolling rack, 61
rounder, 61
rude, 40
(to) ruin, 52
(to) run (in an ad), 4
(to) run smoothly, 112
rust, 90

S

safe, 49
safety, 73
sale item, 61
sales associate, 16
sales floor, 61
sales technique, 16
salesclerk, 16
salesperson, 13
saleswoman, 18
sample, 100
sanitary, 76
satisfaction, 42
satisfied, 42
scam, 30
scanner, 1
(to) schedule, 112
schedule, 112
scheduling, 112
screen, 88
(to) scroll (down or up), 90
seasonal, 4
second, 1
security guard, 49
selection, 16
(to) sell out, 18
(to) send, 18
sensor, 25
(to) separate, 61
service, 4
(to) set, 49
(to) set off, 49
(to) set up, 4
shelf, 13
shift, 112
shipment, 64
(to) shoot, 6
(to) shoot out, 52
(to) shop, 4

shoplifter, 49
shopper, 1
short, 30
shorthanded, 78
(to) show, 13
side, 61
(to) sign, 1
signature, 28
silk, 37
sink, 73
sir, 1
(to) size, 61
size, 13
(to) slip, 73
slot, 28
smart, 16
soap, 76
sofa, 90
soft, 64
solvent, 78
(to) sort, 18
(to) sound, 6
(to) sound like, 30
sparkling, 76
special, 1
specific, 64
(to) spell, 85
(to) split, 52
(to) split up, 13
sporting goods, 49
(to) stack, 66
staff, 16
staff development, 109
stall, 76
stamp, 25
(to) stand back, 73
(to) steal, 49
still, 78
(to) stock, 76
stock, 61
stock clerk, 61
stock purchase plan, 109
stockroom, 64
store, 1
(to) straighten, 18

strength, 100
striped, 13
stupid, 54
style, 13
(to) submit, 85
(to) succeed, 102
successful, 97
supervisor, 28
supply cabinet, 78
support, 109
suspect, 28
suspicious, 52
sweater, 18
(to) switch, 52
sympathetic, 40
system, 85

T

T-stand, 61
tactful, 88
tag, 52
(to) take (pictures), 6
(to) take care of, 49
(to) take off, 49
(to) take orders, 88
take pride in . . ., 102
(to) talk into, 25
tax, 1
tax-deferred savings plan, 109
team, 4
temporary, 102
ten, (a), 30
terminal, 88
terrific, 4
thanks to you, 4
That comes to . . ., 30
That's not a bad idea., 25
the sky's the limit, 109
theft, 52
thief, 52
(to) think so, 18
though, 1
timepiece, 54
to-do list, 4

toilet, 76
toilet seat cover, 76
toilet tissue, 76
tone, 40
toothbrush, 1
top (adjective), 54
top (noun), 18
top-notch, 109
total, 1
(to) touch, 16
towel, 66
trailer, 66
training, 37
transaction, 28
trash, 66
tray, 28
tricky, 66
(to) trip, 73
trip, 25
trouble, 25
truck, 64
(to) try on, 13
turtleneck, 90
tweed, 90
type, 64

U

unadvertised, 1
undercover security officer, 49
uneven exchange, 37
unit, 112
(to) unload, 64
(to) unplug, 73
unusual, 30
(to) unwrap, 64
up-to-date, 73
upset, 114
urinal, 76

V

(to) vacuum, 78
vacuum, 78
valid, 112

valuable, 66
vendor, 61
victim, 30
video, 66
videotape, 54
visually appealing, 112
vitamin, 85
voice, 73
(to) void, 25
voided, 25

W

warning, 52
warranty, 6
waste container, 76
(to) watch, 18
watch, 54
waterfall rack, 61
weakness, 100
weekend, 18
weight, 90
Why don't you . . . ?, 18
willingness, 100
wood, 66
wool, 37
(to) work (one's way up), 109
workout clothes, 85
Wow!, 42
(to) wrap, 73
wrong, 25

Y

You sold me on it., 6
You're absolutely right., 54
You've got it., 85

Z

zoom lens, 6